cybersecurity Bible

Comprehensive Handbook Guide to Become Cybersecurity Expert, how to Detect and Prevent and also Manage Cyber Threats Mastering Digital Asset Protection

by

Preston T. Davis

Copyright ©

By Preston T. Davis 2024. All rights reserved.

Table of content

Introduction

Welcome to Cybersecurity

Hello, and welcome to the fascinating world of cybersecurity! You might wonder, "What is cybersecurity, and why should I care about it?" Well, you're in the right place to find out. This book will explore the ins and outs of staying safe in the digital world. And don't worry, we'll keep it fun and easy to understand. So, let's dive right in!

What is Cybersecurity?

Cybersecurity might sound scary, but it's pretty simple once you break it down. Let's start by understanding what the word means. "Cyber" refers to anything related to computers, technology, and the internet. "Security" means being safe from danger or harm. So, when we put those two words together, "cybersecurity" means keeping everything related to computers, technology, and the internet safe and secure.

Imagine you're building a sandcastle at the beach. You work hard to create tall towers, strong walls, and maybe even a moat. But then you realize you must protect your sandcastle from the waves and other kids who might accidentally knock it down. You build barriers and maybe even dig an enormous moat to keep your castle safe. In the world of technology, cybersecurity is like those barriers and moats. It's about creating defenses to protect our information, devices, and ourselves from various threats.

But what exactly are we protecting ourselves from? Good question! The digital world has many potential dangers, like hackers, viruses, and scams. Like in real life, where you lock your doors to keep your home safe, we must also take steps to secure our digital lives.

Why is Cybersecurity Important?

Now that we know cybersecurity let's talk about why it's so important. In today's world, we use technology for almost everything. We go online to chat with friends, play games, do homework, shop, and so much more. With so much of our lives happening online, it's crucial to ensure we stay safe while doing it.

1. Protecting Personal Information

One of the main reasons cybersecurity is essential is because it helps protect our personal information. Think about all the information you share online: your name, your birthday, your address, and even your photos. It's all personal information that you wouldn't want strangers to have access to. Cybersecurity helps protect this information from people who might try to steal it and use it for bad things.

For example, have you ever heard of identity theft? It's when someone steals your personal information and pretends to be you. They might try to use your information to open bank accounts, make purchases, or even commit crimes. It's a severe problem, but you can help protect yourself with good cybersecurity practices.

2. Keeping Devices Secure

Another vital reason for cybersecurity is to keep our devices safe. Our computers, tablets, and smartphones are like digital treasure chests filled with valuable information. We use these devices to store our photos, work, games, and more. Hackers who enter your device can steal or destroy all that information.

Imagine having a diary where you write down all your thoughts and secrets. You wouldn't want someone to sneak in and read it. The same goes for your digital devices. Cybersecurity helps ensure that only you and the people you trust can access the information on your devices.

3. Avoiding Scams and Fraud

The internet is a beautiful place full of amazing things, but it's also home to people who try to trick others. Scams and fraud are shared online and can be tricky to spot. Cybersecurity teaches us how to recognize these scams and avoid falling for them.

For instance, you might receive an email that looks like it's from your favorite game, asking you to log in to claim a prize. But it could be a trick to steal your password! Learning about cybersecurity helps you identify these fake emails and stay safe from scammers.

4. Protecting Our Future

Technology will play a massive role in our lives as we grow up. Cybersecurity is critical because it helps us build good habits that will keep us safe now and in the future. By learning how to protect ourselves online, we're also learning how to protect our future selves from new and evolving threats.

Imagine you're learning to ride a bike. At first, you use training wheels to help you balance and stay safe. As you get better, you don't need the training wheels anymore, but you still remember the skills you learned. Cybersecurity is like those skills. The things we know now will help us stay safe, even as the digital world changes and grows.

5. Staying Safe While Having Fun

Lastly, cybersecurity is essential because it allows us to enjoy the internet without worrying about getting into trouble. When we know how to stay safe online, we can focus on having fun, learning new things, and connecting with friends. It's like knowing how to swim to enjoy the pool without worrying about drowning.

By understanding cybersecurity, we can confidently explore the internet, knowing that we have the tools and knowledge to protect ourselves from harm.

Let's Get Started!

Now that you have a basic understanding of cybersecurity and its importance, you can start your journey into digital safety. Throughout this book, we'll cover everything you need to know to keep yourself, your information, and your devices safe. We'll learn about creating strong passwords, recognizing scams, securing our devices, and more.

Remember, cybersecurity isn't just for experts. It's for everyone, and that includes you! With the proper knowledge and tools, you can become a cybersecurity hero, protecting yourself and helping others stay safe online.

So, let's get started on this exciting adventure together. By the end of this book, you'll be a cybersecurity pro, ready to navigate the digital world with confidence and ease. Let's dive into the first chapter and start building our cybersecurity skills!

cybersecurity

Chapter 1

Understanding the Internet

What is the Internet?

Welcome to our first chapter, where we'll explore the magical world of the internet! The internet is like a vast, invisible web that connects millions of computers all around the world. It allows us to send and receive information, talk to friends, watch videos, play games, and more.

But how does it all work? Let's break it down.

1. The Basics of the Internet

Think of the internet as a giant city with many roads connecting different places. Each place in the town represents a computer or a server. When you use your computer or phone to go online, you're like a car driving on these roads to reach different destinations.

- Websites: Websites are like buildings in this city. Each website has a unique address called a URL (like www.example.com) that helps you find it.

- Servers: Servers are special computers that store all the information and files that makeup websites. When you visit a website, your computer asks the server to send it the information it needs to display the site.

- Internet Service Providers (I.S.P.s): I.S.P.s are like highways and roads that connect everything. They provide the connection that lets your computer or phone access the internet.

2. How the Internet Works

When you open your web browser and type in a website's address, here's what happens:

- Your computer sends a request through your I.S.P. to find the website's server.

- The server receives the request and returns the information needed to display the website.

- Your computer receives the information and shows you the website on your screen.

It's like sending a letter to a friend and getting a reply, but it happens quickly—often in just a few seconds!

The World of Cybersecurity

Now that we have a basic understanding of the internet, let's dive deeper into cybersecurity. Cybersecurity is all about protecting our digital city from dangers like hackers, viruses, and scams.

1. What is Cybersecurity?

As mentioned in the introduction, cybersecurity keeps everything related to computers, technology, and the internet safe and secure. It's like having a security system for your home but for your digital life.

2. Common Cyber Threats

There are many different types of cyber threats that we need to protect ourselves from. Here are a few of the most common ones:

- Hackers: Hackers try to break into computers and networks to steal information or cause damage. Think of them like digital burglars.

- Viruses and Malware: Viruses and malware are harmful programs that can infect your computer, just like germs can make you sick. They can delete files, steal information, and cause your computer to stop working correctly.

- Scams and Phishing: Scammers trick you into giving them your personal information, like passwords or credit card numbers. Phishing is a type of scam where someone pretends to be a trustworthy source, like your bank or a friend, to steal your information.

Keeping Your Information Safe

1. Protecting Personal Information

Your personal information is like a treasure chest filled with valuable items. It includes your name, address, phone number, and password. Keeping this information safe is one of the most essential parts of cybersecurity.

- Sharing Safely: Be careful about what you share online. Only give your personal information to websites and people you trust. If a website asks for information that doesn't seem right, it's better to be safe and not share.

- Using Strong Passwords: A strong password is like a lock on your treasure chest. It should be hard for others to guess but easy for you to remember. Use a mix of letters, numbers, and symbols to create strong passwords.

2. Creating Strong Passwords

Creating strong passwords is one of the simplest yet most effective ways to protect your personal information. Here's how you can make sure your passwords are strong:

- Length and Complexity: Your password should be at least eight characters long and include a mix of uppercase and lowercase letters, numbers, and special characters like! @, or.

- Avoid Common Words: Avoid easily guessable words like "password" or "123456." Instead, think of a phrase or a combination of words only you would know.

- Use Different Passwords: Don't use the same password for multiple accounts. If one account gets hacked, others could be at risk, too. Using different passwords for different accounts keeps them all more secure.

Safe Browsing

1. Browsing the Internet Safely

When browsing the internet, staying safe and avoiding dangerous websites is essential. Here are some tips to help you browse safely:

- Use Trusted Websites: Stick to websites you know and trust. If you need clarification on a website, ask a trusted adult for help.

- Look for HTTPS: Websites that start with "https://" are more secure than those that begin with "http://." The "s" stands for secure. Look for a padlock icon in the address bar to ensure the site is safe.

- Avoid Clicking on Unknown Links: Be careful about clicking on links in emails, messages, or websites you don't trust. They could lead to dangerous websites or download harmful files.

2. Recognizing Dangerous Websites

Not all websites are safe; some might trick you into giving away your personal information or downloading malware. Here are some signs of a dangerous website:

- Pop-Ups and Ads: Be wary of websites with many pop-ups and ads, especially if they ask you to click on them or enter personal information.

- Spelling and Grammar Errors: Many dangerous websites have spelling and grammar mistakes. It might be unsafe if a website looks unprofessional or poorly written.

- Too Good to Be True: If a website offers deals or prizes that seem too good, they probably are. Be cautious and avoid giving away personal information.

Understanding Malware

1. What is Malware?

Malware is short for "malicious software." It's any program or file designed to harm your computer or steal your information. Different types of malwares include viruses, worms, trojans, and ransomware.

- Viruses: Viruses attach themselves to files and programs. When you open the infected file, the virus spreads and can damage your computer.

- Worms: Worms are similar to viruses but can spread without your help. They move through networks and can infect many computers quickly.

- Trojans: Trojans look like safe programs, but once you install them, they can steal information or harm your computer.

- Ransomware: Ransomware locks your computer or files and demands money to unlock them. It's like a digital hostage situation.

2. Protecting Against Malware

Keeping your devices safe from malware is crucial. Here are some steps you can take to protect yourself:

- Use Antivirus Software: Antivirus software can find and remove malware from your computer. Make sure to keep your antivirus software up to date.

- Update Your Software: Software updates often include security fixes. Keep your operating system, apps, and antivirus software updated to stay protected.

- Be Cautious with Downloads: Only download files and programs from trusted sources. Avoid downloading anything from unknown or suspicious websites.

Safe Communication

1. Email Safety

Emails are a common way for scammers to try and trick you. Here's how to stay safe when using email:

- Check the Sender: Always check who the email is from. Be cautious if you don't recognize the sender or the email address looks strange.

- Avoid Clicking on Links: Don't click on links or download attachments from unknown or suspicious emails. They could lead to dangerous websites or download malware.

- Look for Red Flags: Watch out for emails that ask for personal information or have spelling and grammar mistakes. If something doesn't seem right, it isn't.

2. Social Media Safety

Social media is a great way to stay connected with friends, but keeping safe is essential. Here are some tips:

- Privacy Settings: Use the privacy settings on social media to control who can see your information and posts. Only share with people you trust.

- Be Careful What You Share: Don't share personal information like your address, phone number, or passwords. Be mindful of what you post and who can see it.

- Recognize Fake Profiles: Be cautious of friend requests from people you don't know. Fake profiles can be used to gather personal information or send harmful links.

Understanding Phishing

1. What is Phishing?

Phishing is a scam where someone pretends to be a trustworthy source to steal your personal information. It might send fake email messages or create fake websites to trick you.

- How Phishing Works: A phishing scam usually involves a fake email or message that looks like it's from a trusted source, like your bank or a popular website. The message will ask you to click a link and enter your personal information.

- Common Phishing Scams: Some phishing scams include fake emails from banks, online stores, or friends. They might ask you to update your account information, claim a prize, or verify your identity.

2. Protecting Against Phishing

Here's how you can protect yourself from phishing scams:

- Don't Click on Suspicious Links: If you receive an email or message asking for personal information, don't click on any links. Instead, go directly to the website by typing the URL into your browser.

- Verify the Source: Verify the source if you need an email or message clarification. Contact the company or person directly using a trusted method, like their official website or phone number.

- Report Phishing Attempts: If you receive a phishing email or message,

Please report it to the company it's pretending to be from. Most companies have a way to report phishing attempts.

Keeping Devices Secure

1. Securing Your Computer

Your computer is a treasure chest of information, so keeping it secure is important. Here are some tips:

- Use Strong Passwords: Always use strong, unique passwords for your computer and accounts.

- Update Your Software: Keep your operating system, antivirus, and other software up to date to protect against security vulnerabilities.

- Enable a Firewall: A firewall helps block unauthorized access to your computer. Make sure your firewall is enabled and properly configured.

2. Securing Your Smartphone and Tablet

Smartphones and tablets are just as crucial for keeping secure. Here's how:

- Use a Passcode or Biometric Lock: Always lock your device with a passcode, fingerprint, or facial recognition.

- Download Apps from Trusted Sources: Only download apps from trusted sources like the official app store for your device.

- Be Careful with Public Wi-Fi: Avoid using public Wi-Fi for sensitive activities, like online banking. If you need public Wi-Fi, use a virtual private network (VPN) to encrypt your connection.

Learning About Data Privacy

1. What is Data Privacy?

Data privacy is all about protecting your personal information from being shared or accessed without your permission. It's important because your personal information is valuable and can be used in harmful ways if it falls into the wrong hands.

- Why Data Privacy Matters: Protecting your data helps prevent identity theft, financial fraud, and other types of cybercrime. It also enables you to maintain control over your personal information.

2. Safe Online Shopping

Shopping online is convenient, but it's essential to do it safely. Here are some tips:

- Shop on Trusted Websites: Only shop on websites you know and trust. Look for **"https://"** in the URL and a padlock icon to ensure the site is secure.

- Use Secure Payment Methods: Use secure payment methods, like credit cards or trusted payment services. Avoid using debit cards or direct bank transfers.

- Keep Your Information Private: Don't share unnecessary personal information. Only provide what's needed to complete your purchase.

Cyberbullying and Online Safety

1. What is Cyberbullying?

Cyberbullying is when someone uses technology to harass, threaten, or embarrass another person. It can happen through emails, messages, social media, or other online platforms.

- Recognizing Cyberbullying: Cyberbullying can take many forms, like mean messages, spreading false news, or posting embarrassing photos. It's important to recognize it and know how to respond.

- How to Respond to Cyberbullying: Tell a trusted adult if you or someone you know is being cyberbullied. Don't respond to the bully; keep evidence of the bullying to show to the adult.

2. Staying Safe Online

Here are some general tips to help you stay safe online:

- Think Before You Share: Consider what you share and who can see it. Once something is online, it's hard to take it back.

- Be Kind and Respectful: Treat others with kindness and respect online, just like in real life. Don't say or do anything you wouldn't want someone to say or do to you.

- Talk to Trusted Adults: If you ever feel uncomfortable or unsure about something online, talk to a trusted adult. They can help you navigate the situation and stay safe.

By understanding and practicing cybersecurity, you take the necessary steps to protect yourself digitally. Remember, staying safe online is about being aware, making intelligent choices, and always thinking about how to keep your information and devices secure. Now that you've learned the basics, you're ready to dive deeper into cybersecurity and become a digital safety pro. **Let's continue this journey together and explore even more ways to stay safe and secure online!**

Chapter 2

The World of Cybersecurity

What is Cybersecurity?

Welcome to the second chapter of our journey into the world of cybersecurity. Now that you understand the internet and its workings, it's time to dive deeper into cybersecurity and why it's so important. We'll also explore some common cyber threats you must be aware of.

Definition and Importance

Cybersecurity is about protecting your computer, data, and yourself from digital dangers. Think of it as a set of rules and practices that help keep you safe online. Just like you lock your doors at home to keep out burglars, cybersecurity enables you to lock your digital doors to keep out hackers and other cyber threats.

But why is cybersecurity so critical? Let's break it down:

1. Protecting Personal Information

In today's world, we share a lot of personal information online. It includes things like our names, addresses, phone numbers, and photos. If this information falls into the wrong hands, it can be used to steal your identity, commit fraud, or cause other serious problems. Cybersecurity helps keep your personal information safe and secure.

2. Maintaining Privacy

Everyone has a right to Privacy in the real world and online. Cybersecurity practices help protect your Privacy by ensuring that your personal information is only accessible to you and the people you trust. It's essential when using social media, online banking, and other services that require personal information.

3. Preventing Financial Loss

Cybercrime can lead to significant financial loss. For example, if a hacker gains access to your bank account or credit card information, they could steal your money or make unauthorized purchases. Cybersecurity measures help prevent these financial crimes by protecting sensitive information.

4. Ensuring Safe Communication

We use the internet to communicate with friends, family, and colleagues. These communications must be secure through email, social media, or messaging apps. Cybersecurity helps ensure that your messages and conversations remain private and aren't intercepted by hackers.

5. Protecting Businesses and Organizations

Cybersecurity isn't just critical for individuals; it's also crucial for businesses and organizations. Companies store sensitive information, including customer data, financial records, and trade secrets. A cyber-attack on a business can lead to data breaches, economic losses, and damage to the company's reputation. By implementing strong cybersecurity practices, businesses can protect their data and ensure their operations run smoothly.

Common Cyber Threats

Now that we understand why cybersecurity is essential, let's explore some common cyber threats we need to protect ourselves from. These threats can come in many forms, and it's necessary to recognize them so that you can stay safe online.

1. Hackers

Hackers use their computer skills to break into systems and networks. Some hackers do this for fun or to prove their skills, while others do it for malicious reasons, such as stealing information or causing damage. Hackers can target individuals, businesses, and even government organizations.

Types of Hackers:

- **White Hat Hackers:** These are ethical hackers who use their skills to help improve security. They often work with companies to find and fix security vulnerabilities.

- **Black Hat Hackers:** These are the bad guys. Black hat hackers use their skills for illegal activities, such as stealing data or spreading malware.

- **Gray Hat Hackers:** These hackers fall somewhere in between. They might break into systems without permission but don't have malicious intent. Instead, they might expose vulnerabilities to encourage the system owner to improve security.

2. Malware

Malware is short for **"malicious software."** This software is designed to harm your computer or steal your information. There are many types of malwares, each with its methods and goals.

Types of Malware:

- **Viruses:** A virus is a malware that attaches itself to a legitimate file or program. When you open the infected file, the virus spreads to other files and programs on your computer, causing damage.

- **Worms:** Worms are similar to viruses but don't need to attach themselves to a file. Instead, they spread through networks, infecting multiple computers.

- **Trojans:** Named after the Trojan Horse from Greek mythology, a Trojan is a type of malware that disguises itself as a legitimate program. Once you install it, the Trojan can steal your information or give hackers access to your computer.

- **Ransomware:** Ransomware is malware that locks your files or entire computer, demanding a ransom to unlock them. It's like a digital kidnapping of your data.

3. Phishing

Phishing is a scam where someone pretends to be a trustworthy source to trick you into giving away your personal information. Phishing scams often come in emails, messages, or fake websites that look legitimate.

- How Phishing Works:

- Fake Emails: You might receive an email that looks like it's from your bank, a popular website, or even a friend. The email usually asks you to click a link and enter your personal information.

- Fake Websites: The link in the phishing email might take you to a fake website that looks just like the real thing. Once you enter your information, the scammers can steal and use it maliciously.

4. Social Engineering

Social engineering is a tactic used by cybercriminals to manipulate people into giving away their personal information or performing specific actions. Unlike other cyber threats that rely on technology, social engineering relies on human interaction and psychology.

- Types of Social Engineering:

- Pretexting: The attacker creates a fake scenario (or pretext) to trick you into giving away information. For example, they might pretend to be a customer service representative asking for your account details.

- Baiting: The attacker offers something enticing to lure you into a trap. For example, they might leave a USB drive labelled "Confidential" in a public place, hoping someone will pick it up and plug it into their computer.

- Tailgating: The attacker follows someone into a secure area by pretending to be authorized. For example, they might pretend to remember their access card and ask someone to open the door.

5. Denial-of-Service (DoS) Attacks

A Denial-of-Service (DoS) attack is an attempt to make a website or online service unavailable by overwhelming it with traffic. It can cause the website to slow down or crash, making it inaccessible to users.

- How DoS Attacks Work:

- Flooding: The attacker sends massive traffic to the target website, overwhelming its servers and causing it to crash.

- Distributed Denial-of-Service (DDoS): In a DDoS attack, the attacker uses multiple computers (often part of a botnet) to flood the target with traffic. It makes the attack even more powerful and more challenging to stop.

6. Spyware

Spyware is malware that secretly monitors your computer activity and collects information without your knowledge. It can track your keystrokes, capture screenshots, and even record your browsing history.

- How Spyware Works:

- Keyloggers: Keyloggers are spyware that records every keystroke you make. It can include usernames, passwords, and other sensitive information.

- Adware: Adware is a type of spyware that displays unwanted advertisements on your computer. It can also track your browsing habits to show you targeted ads.

7. Man-in-the-Middle (MitM) Attacks

In a Man-in-the-Middle (MitM) attack, the attacker intercepts and alters communication between two parties without their knowledge. It can allow the attacker to steal information, eavesdrop on conversations, or even change the content of the communication.

- How MitM Attacks Work:

- Eavesdropping: To steal information, the attacker intercepts communication between two parties, such as an email or a chat message.

- Session Hijacking: The attacker takes over a user's session on a website or service, allowing them to access the user's account and perform actions as if they were the user.

8. Zero-Day Exploits

A zero-day exploit is a cyber-attack that takes advantage of a previously unknown vulnerability in software or hardware. Because the vulnerability is unknown, there is no defense against it, making zero-day exploits particularly dangerous.

- How Zero-Day Exploits Work:

- Finding Vulnerabilities: Cybercriminals search for vulnerabilities in software and hardware that haven't been discovered or patched by the developers.

- Exploiting Vulnerabilities: Once a vulnerability is noticed, the attacker creates an exploit to exploit it. It can include installing malware, stealing information, or gaining unauthorized access to a system.

Protecting Yourself from Cyber Threats

Now that we know about common cyber threats, we must learn how to protect ourselves. Here are some critical cybersecurity practices that can help keep you safe online:

1. Use Strong Passwords

We've already discussed the importance of strong passwords, but it's worth repeating. Use a mix of letters, numbers, and symbols to create strong, unique passwords for each account. Avoid using common words or quickly guessable information, like your name or birthday.

2. Keep Your Software Updated

Software updates often include critical security patches that fix vulnerabilities. Keep your operating system, web browser, antivirus software, and other programs up to date to protect against the latest threats.

3. Be Cautious with Emails and Messages

Be wary of emails and messages from unknown senders, especially if they ask for personal information or include links and attachments. If

If something seems suspicious, don't click on any links or download any files. Instead, verify the sender by contacting them directly through a trusted method.

4. Enable Two-Factor Authentication (2FA)

Two-factor authentication adds an extra layer of security to your accounts by requiring a second form of verification in addition to your password. It could be a code sent to your phone, a fingerprint scan, or another method. Enable 2FA on your important accounts to make them more secure.

5. Use Antivirus and Anti-Malware Software

Antivirus and anti-malware software can help detect and remove malicious programs from your computer. Keep your antivirus software current and run regular scans to check for threats.

6. Be Careful with Public Wi-Fi

Public Wi-Fi networks can be less secure than your home network, making it easier for cybercriminals to intercept your data. Avoid using public Wi-Fi for sensitive activities like online banking. If you need public Wi-Fi, use a virtual private network (VPN) to encrypt your connection.

7. Back Up Your Data

Regularly back up your important files to an external hard drive or a cloud storage service. This way, if your computer is infected with malware or you experience a hardware failure, you won't lose your data.

8. Educate Yourself and Others

Stay informed about the latest cybersecurity threats and best practices. Please share your knowledge with friends and family to help them stay safe online.

Following these cybersecurity practices can protect you from common cyber threats and help you enjoy a safer online experience. Cybersecurity is an ongoing process, and staying vigilant is critical to securing your digital life.

Let's Continue

Chapter 3

Keeping Your Information Safe

Welcome to Chapter 3! Now that we've explored cybersecurity and its importance, it's time to dive into the specifics of keeping your information safe. We'll discuss protecting your personal information, creating strong passwords, and avoiding common cyber threats. *Let's get started!*

Protecting Personal Information

Your personal information is like a treasure chest filled with valuable items. It includes your name, address, phone number, and password. Keeping this information safe is one of the most essential parts of cybersecurity.

1. Understanding Personal Information

First, let's talk about what personal information is. Personal information is any data that can identify you as an individual. This can include:

1. **Full Name:** Your first and last name.
2. **Address:** Where you live.
3. **Phone Number:** Your contact number.
4. **Email Address:** Your email.
5. **Birthdate:** Your date of birth.
6. **Social Security Number:** A unique number used for identification in many countries.
7. **Financial Information:** Bank account numbers, credit card numbers, etc.
8. **Passwords:** Keys to access your accounts.
9. **Photos and Videos:** Personal images and recordings.

Why is this information valuable? Because it can be used to steal your identity, commit fraud, or gain unauthorized access to your accounts. That's why it's essential to keep it secure.

2. Sharing Safely

Be cautious about what you share online. Only give your personal information to websites and people you trust. Here are some tips to help you share information safely:

- Think Before You Share: Always consider whether the information you share is necessary and who will see it.

- Check Privacy Settings: Use the privacy settings on social media and other websites to control who can see your information.

- Be Wary of Unknown Sources: Don't share personal information with strangers or on untrusted websites.

- Limit Personal Details: Only share the necessary details. For example, a website might need your name and email address but not your phone number or address.

3. Recognizing Phishing Scams

Phishing scams are a common way for cybercriminals to try to steal personal information. These scams often come in the form of fake emails, messages, or websites that look legitimate. Here's how to recognize and avoid phishing scams:

- Check the sender: Look at the sender's email address or phone number. If it looks suspicious or doesn't match the official contact details of the organization, be cautious.

- Look for Red Flags: Phishing messages often contain spelling and grammar mistakes, urgent language, or suspicious links. If something seems off, it probably is.

- Verify the Source: If you receive a message asking for personal information, contact the organization using a trusted method to verify the request.

- Don't Click on Suspicious Links: Hover over links to see the URL before clicking. If the URL looks strange or doesn't match the official website, don't click.

4. Using Secure Websites

When sharing personal information online, make sure you're using secure websites. Here's how to identify safe websites:

- Look for HTTPS: Secure websites start with **"https://"** instead of **"http://."** The "s" stands for secure.

- Check for a Padlock Icon: Look for a padlock icon in your browser's address bar. This indicates that the website is using a secure connection.

- Avoid Public Wi-Fi: Don't share personal information over public Wi-Fi networks, as they can be less secure. If you need public Wi-Fi, use a VPN to encrypt your connection.

Creating Strong Passwords

Creating strong passwords is one of the simplest yet most effective ways to protect your personal information. Here's how you can make sure your passwords are strong and secure:

1. What Makes a Strong Password?

A strong password should be:

- Long: At least 12 characters long.

- Complex: Includes a mix of uppercase and lowercase letters, numbers, and special characters like, !, @, or.

- Unique: Different from your other passwords.

- Not Guessable: Avoid using easily guessable information like your name, birthday, or common words.

2. Tips for Creating Strong Passwords

Here are some tips to help you create strong passwords:

- Use a Passphrase: Create a passphrase by combining random words, like **"BlueAppleCar$Tree."** This is easier to remember and still secure.

- Mix It Up: Use letters, numbers, and special characters. For example, "P@ssw0rd!" is more secure than "password."

- Avoid Common Patterns: Don't use patterns like "123456" or "abide." These are easily guessable by hackers.

- Use Password Managers: Password managers can help you create and store strong, unique passwords for each account.

3. Changing Your Passwords Regularly

Changing your passwords regularly is good practice, especially for important accounts like email and online banking. Here's why:

- Reduce Risk: If a hacker gains access to one of your passwords, regularly changing your password can reduce the risk of unauthorized access.

- Protect Against Data Breaches: Data breaches happen when hackers steal large amounts of data, including passwords. Regularly changing your passwords helps protect you if your data is compromised in a breach.

4. Two-Factor Authentication (2FA)

Two-factor authentication (2FA) adds an extra layer of security to your accounts. It requires a second form of verification in addition to your password. Here's how it works:

- Something You Know: Your password.

- Something You Have: A code sent to your phone, a fingerprint scan, or another method.

By enabling 2FA on your important accounts, you can make them much more secure. Even if someone gets your password, they will need the second verification form to access your account.

Avoiding Common Cyber Threats

In addition to creating strong passwords and protecting your personal information, it's essential to be aware of common cyber threats and how to avoid them. Here are some critical threats to watch out for:

1. Malware

Malware is malicious software designed to harm your computer or steal your information. Different types of malware include viruses, worms, trojans, and ransomware. Here's how to protect yourself:

- Use Antivirus Software: Antivirus software can detect and remove malware from your computer. Make sure to keep it up to date.

- Avoid Downloading Unknown Files: Only download files from trusted sources. Be cautious of email attachments and downloads from untrusted websites.

- Keep Your Software Updated: Software updates often include security patches that fix vulnerabilities. Keep your operating system and software up to date.

2. Social Engineering

Social engineering is a tactic used by cybercriminals to manipulate people into giving away their personal information. Here are some common social engineering tactics and how to avoid them:

- Pretexting: The attacker creates a fake scenario to trick you into giving away information. Always verify the identity of the person asking for information.

- Baiting: The attacker offers something enticing to lure you into a trap. Be cautious of offers that seem too good to be true.

- Tailgating: The attacker follows someone into a secure area. Only let strangers into secure areas with proper authorization.

3. Denial-of-Service (DoS) Attacks

A Denial-of-Service (DoS) attack is an attempt to make a website or online service unavailable by overwhelming it with traffic. Here's how to protect yourself:

- Use Strong Passwords: Ensure your accounts have strong passwords to prevent unauthorized access.

- Enable Security Features: Use security features like firewalls and intrusion detection systems to protect your network.

- Monitor Traffic: Monitor your network traffic for any unusual activity that might indicate a DoS attack.

4. Spyware

Spyware is software that secretly monitors your computer activity and collects information without your knowledge. Here's how to protect yourself:

- Use Anti-Spyware Software: Anti-spyware software can detect and remove spyware from your computer.

- Be Cautious of Free Software: Some free software can contain spyware. Only download software from trusted sources.

- Keep Your Software Updated: Regularly update your operating system and software to protect against spyware.

5. Man-in-the-Middle (MitM) Attacks

In a Man-in-the-Middle (MitM) attack, the attacker intercepts and alters communication between two parties without their knowledge. Here's how to protect yourself:

- Use Encryption: Encryption helps protect your communication by making it unreadable to anyone who intercepts it. Use encrypted messaging apps and secure websites (HTTPS).

- Avoid Public Wi-Fi: Public Wi-Fi networks can be less secure. Use a VPN to encrypt your connection if you need to use public Wi-Fi.

- Verify Websites: Ensure you're on the correct website before entering personal information. Look for HTTPS and the padlock icon in the address bar.

Safe Browsing Practices

Browsing the internet safely is crucial for protecting your personal information and avoiding cyber threats. Here are some safe browsing practices to follow:

1. Use Secure Websites

When browsing the internet, make sure you're using secure websites. Here's how to identify secure websites:

- Look for HTTPS: Secure websites start with **"https://"** instead of **"http://."** The "s" stands for secure.

- Check for a Padlock Icon: Look for a padlock icon in your browser's address bar. This indicates that the website is using a secure connection.

2. Avoid Clicking on Unknown Links

Be cautious about clicking on links in emails, messages, or websites you don't trust. Here's why:

- Phishing Scams: Phishing scams often use links to direct you to fake websites that look legitimate. These websites are designed to steal your personal information.

- Malware: Some links can download malware onto your computer. Only click on links from trusted sources.

3. Use a Secure Web Browser

A secure web browser can help protect you from cyber threats. Here's what to look for in a secure browser:

- Security Features: Look for features like pop-up blockers, anti-phishing protection, and sandboxing (which isolates web pages to prevent malware from spreading).

- Regular Updates: Choose a browser that receives regular updates to fix security vulnerabilities.

- Privacy Controls: Look for privacy controls that allow you to manage cookies block trackers, and control what information websites can collect.

4. Be Cautious with Downloads

Only download files and programs from trusted sources. Here's why:

- Malware: Downloading files from untrusted sources can result in malware infections. Make sure the website is reputable before downloading anything.

- Verify Files: Verify the file type before downloading. It could be malware if you expect a document, but the file type is .exe (an executable file).

5. Use Ad Blockers

Ad blockers can help prevent malicious ads from appearing on websites. Here's how they work:

- Block Ads: Ad blockers prevent ads from loading on web pages. This can help protect you from malicious ads that contain malware or phishing links.

- Improve Privacy: Ad blockers can also block tracking scripts that collect information about your browsing habits.

Keeping Devices Secure

In addition to protecting your personal information and practicing safe browsing, keeping your devices secure is essential. Here are some tips for securing your computers, smartphones, and tablets:

1. Securing Your Computer

Your computer is a treasure chest of information, so keeping it secure is important. Here are some tips:

- Use Strong Passwords: Always use strong, unique passwords for your computer and accounts.

- Update Your Software: Keep your operating system, antivirus, and other software up to date to protect against security vulnerabilities.

- Enable a Firewall: A firewall helps block unauthorized access to your computer. Make sure your firewall is enabled and properly configured.

2. Securing Your Smartphone and Tablet

Smartphones and tablets are just as crucial for keeping secure. Here's how:

- Use a Passcode or Biometric Lock: Always lock your device with a passcode, fingerprint, or facial recognition.

- Download Apps from Trusted Sources: Only download apps from trusted sources like the official app store for your device.

- Be Careful with Public Wi-Fi: Avoid using public Wi-Fi for sensitive activities, like online banking. If you need public Wi-Fi, use a virtual private network (VPN) to encrypt your connection.

3. Using Encryption

Encryption helps protect your data by making it unreadable to anyone who intercepts it. Here's how to use Encryption:

- Encrypt Your Device: Many smartphones and computers have built-in encryption features. Enable Encryption in your device's settings to protect your data.

- Use Encrypted Messaging Apps: Use messaging apps that offer end-to-end Encryption, like Signal or WhatsApp, to protect your conversations.

4. Regular Backups

Regularly backing up your essential files helps protect against data loss. Here's how to do it:

- External Hard Drive: An external hard drive will back up your files. Make sure to keep the hard drive in a safe place.

- Cloud Storage: Use a cloud storage service to back up your files online. Make sure to choose a reputable service with solid security features.

5. Securing Your Network

Securing your home network helps protect all the devices connected to it. Here's how:

- Use a Strong Wi-Fi Password: Ensure your Wi-Fi network is protected with a strong password. Avoid using easily guessable passwords like "password" or "123456."

- Change Default Settings: Change your router's default username and password. Hackers often target default settings to gain access to networks.

- Enable Network Encryption: Use WPA3 encryption for your Wi-Fi network. This is the latest and most secure encryption standard.

Following these cybersecurity practices can protect you from common cyber threats and help you enjoy a safer online experience. Cybersecurity is an ongoing process; staying vigilant is critical to securing your digital life.

Avoiding Scams

Chapter 4

Recognizing and Avoiding Scams

Welcome in this chapter, we'll explore the different types of scams that cybercriminals use to trick people and how you can recognize and avoid them. Understanding these scams is crucial for staying safe online. Let's dive in!

Types of Scams

There are many different types of scams that cybercriminals use to deceive people. Here are some of the most common ones:

1. Phishing Scams

Phishing scams involve cybercriminals pretending to be a trusted entity to steal personal information, such as usernames, passwords, and credit card details. These scams often come in emails, messages, or fake websites that look legitimate.

- Email Phishing: Cybercriminals send fake emails that look like they're from reputable companies, such as banks or online stores. The email often contains a link to a phoney website asking you to enter your personal information.

- Spear Phishing: This is a more targeted form of phishing. Cybercriminals target specific individuals or organizations instead of sending emails to many people. The email is often personalized, making it more convincing.

- Whaling: Whaling targets high-profile individuals, such as C.E.O.s or executives. The email is crafted to look like an important message from a trusted source.

2. Smishing and Vishing

Smishing and vishing are similar to phishing but use different methods.

- Smishing: Smishing involves sending fake text messages that appear to be from trusted sources. The message might contain a link to a phoney website or ask you to reply with personal information.

- Vishing: Vishing involves phone calls where the caller pretends to be from a legitimate organization. They might ask for personal information or get you to perform specific actions, like transferring money.

3. Fake Websites and Online Stores

Cybercriminals create fake websites that look legitimate to trick people into entering their personal information. These websites can be challenging to spot because they often look similar to the real ones.

- Fake Online Stores: These websites look like online stores but are designed to steal your personal and payment information. They might offer products at low prices to lure you in.

- Fake Login Pages: These pages look like the login pages of popular websites, such as social media or email providers. When you enter your username and password, the cybercriminals steal your credentials.

4. Lottery and Prize Scams

Lottery and prize scams involve cybercriminals telling you that you've won a prize or lottery, even though you didn't enter any contest. They might ask for personal information or a payment to claim your prize

- Advance Fee Scams: The cybercriminals ask you to pay a fee in advance to claim your prize. Once you pay the cost, you never hear from them again.

- Personal Information Scams: Instead of asking for money, the scammers ask for personal information, such as your name, address, and bank details.

5. Tech Support Scams

Tech support scams involve cybercriminals pretending to be from a tech support service like Microsoft or Apple. They might call you or send you a pop-up message saying that your computer has a virus and that they need to fix it.

- Phone Calls: The scammer calls you and pretends to be a tech support representative. They might ask for remote access to your computer or for payment to fix the supposed issue.

- Pop-Up Messages: You might see a pop-up message on your computer saying that your system is infected with a virus. The message usually includes a phone number to call for help.

6. Investment and Employment Scams

These scams involve cybercriminals promising high investment returns or offering fake job opportunities to steal your money or personal information.

- Investment Scams: The scammer promises high returns on an investment opportunity that's too good to be true. They might ask for an upfront payment or personal information.

- Employment Scams: The scammer offers you a job, often with high pay and flexible hours. They might ask for personal information or an upfront payment for training or equipment.

How to Recognize Scams

Recognizing scams is the first step in protecting yourself. Here are some tips to help you identify common scams:

1. Check the Sender's Information

Always check the sender's information, such as the email address or phone number. If it looks suspicious or doesn't match the official contact details of the organization, be cautious.

- Email Addresses: Look at the email address closely. Scammers often use addresses similar to legitimate ones but with slight variations.

- Phone Numbers: If you receive a suspicious call, hang up and verify the phone number by contacting the organization directly using their official contact details.

2. Look for Red Flags

Scam messages often contain red flags, such as spelling and grammar mistakes, urgent language, and suspicious links.

- Spelling and Grammar Mistakes: Legitimate organizations usually proofread their messages. If you notice multiple mistakes, be cautious.

- Urgent Language: Scammers often create a sense of urgency to pressure you into acting quickly without thinking. Be wary of messages that demand immediate action.

- Suspicious Links: Hover over links to see the URL before clicking. If the URL looks strange or doesn't match the official website, don't click.

3. Verify the Source

If you receive a message asking for personal information, contact the organization using a trusted method to verify the request.

- Official Websites: Go to the official website by typing the URL into your browser rather than clicking on a link in the message.

- Phone Numbers: Call the organization using the phone number on their official website or your account statement.

4. Be Cautious with Unsolicited Offers

Be cautious of unsolicited offers, especially if they seem too good to be true. Scammers often use attractive offers to lure you in.

- Free Prizes and Lotteries: Be cautions of messages saying you've won a prize or lottery if you didn't enter any contest.

- High Returns on Investments: Be cautious of investment opportunities that promise high returns with little or no risk.

How to Avoid Scams

In addition to recognizing scams, knowing how to avoid them is essential. Here are some tips to help you stay safe:

1. Don't Share Personal Information

Be careful about sharing personal information, especially over the phone or through email and text messages.

- Verify the Request: If you're asking for personal information, verify the request by contacting the organization using a trusted method.

- Limit Sharing: Only share the necessary information and be cautious about what you share online.

2. Use Strong Passwords and Two-Factor Authentication

Using strong passwords and enabling two-factor authentication (2FA) can help protect your accounts from being compromised.

- Strong Passwords: Create strong, unique passwords for each account. Use a mix of letters, numbers, and special characters.

- Two-Factor Authentication: Enable 2FA on your important accounts to add an extra layer of security.

3. Be Cautious with Links and Attachments

Be cautious about clicking links and downloading attachments from emails and messages, especially from unknown senders.

- Verify Links: Hover over links to see the URL before clicking. If the URL looks suspicious, don't click.

- Scan Attachments: Use antivirus software to scan attachments before opening them.

4. Keep Your Software Updated

Keep your operating system, web browser, antivirus software, and other programs up to date to protect against the latest security threats.

- Enable Automatic Updates: Enable automatic updates to ensure your software is always up to date.

- Check for Updates Regularly: Regularly check for updates and install them promptly.

5. Use Security Software

Use antivirus and anti-malware software to protect your devices from malicious programs.

- Regular Scans: Run regular scans to detect and remove malware from your computer.

- Real-Time Protection: Enable real-time protection to prevent malware from being installed on your device.

6. Educate Yourself and Others

Stay informed about the latest scams and cybersecurity threats, and share your knowledge with friends and family to help them stay safe.

- Learn About Scams: Regularly read about new scams and cybersecurity threats to stay informed.

- Share Information: Educate your friends and family about common scams and how to avoid them.

Responding to Scams

Even with the best precautions, you might still encounter scams. Here's how to respond if you think you've been targeted:

1. Don't Respond

If you receive a suspicious email, message, or phone call, wait to respond. Ignore the message and delete it.

- Avoid Clicking Links: Don't click on any links or download attachments from suspicious messages.

- Don't Share Information: Don't share personal information with the sender.

2. Report the Scam

Report the scam to the appropriate authorities, such as your email provider, phone carrier, or government agency.

- Email Providers: Most email providers have a way to report phishing emails. Look for a "Report Phishing" or "Report Spam" option.

- Phone Carriers: Contact your phone carrier to report suspicious calls and messages.

- Government Agencies: Report the scam to a government agency, such as the Federal Trade Commission (F.T.C.) or the Internet Crime Complaint Center (IC3).

3. Change Your Passwords

Change your passwords immediately if you think your accounts have been compromise.

- Create Strong Passwords: Create strong, unique passwords for each account.

- Enable Two-Factor Authentication: Enable 2FA on your important accounts to add an extra layer of security.

4. Monitor Your Accounts

Keep an eye on your accounts for any.

Suspicious activity. If you notice any unauthorized transactions or changes, report them immediately.

- Bank Accounts: Monitor your bank accounts and credit card statements for unauthorized transactions.

- Online Accounts: Check your online accounts for suspicious activity like password changes or new devices.

Safe Communication Practices

Communication is a big part of our online lives, and staying safe is essential. Here are some tips for safe communication:

1. Email Safety

Emails are a common way for scammers to try and trick you. Here's how to stay safe when using email:

- Check the Sender: Always check who the email is from. Be cautious if you don't recognize the sender or the email address looks strange.

- Avoid Clicking on Links: Don't click on links or download attachments from unknown or suspicious emails. They could lead to dangerous websites or download malware.

- Look for Red Flags: Watch out for emails that ask for personal information or have spelling and grammar mistakes. If something seems wrong, it isn't.

2. Social Media Safety

Social media is a great way to stay connected with friends, but keeping safe is essential. Here are some tips:

- Privacy Settings: Use the privacy settings on social media to control who can see your information and posts. Only share with people you trust.

- Be Careful What You Share: Don't share personal information like your address, phone number, or passwords. Be mindful of what you post and who can see it.

- Recognize Fake Profiles: Be cautious of friend requests from people you don't know. Fake profiles can be used to gather personal information or send harmful links.

3. Messaging Apps

Messaging apps are convenient for staying in touch with friends and family, but scammers can also use them. Here's how to stay safe:

- Use Encrypted Apps: Use messaging apps that offer end-to-end Encryption, like Signal or WhatsApp, to protect your conversations.

- Verify Contacts: If you receive a message from someone you don't know, verify their identity before responding. Be cautious of messages that ask for personal information or money.

- Avoid Suspicious Links: Don't click on links from unknown or suspicious messages. They could lead to dangerous websites or download malware.

4. Phone Calls

Phone calls are another standard method used by scammers. Here's how to stay safe:

- Verify the Caller: If you receive a call from an unknown number, verify the caller's identity before sharing any information. Be cautious of calls that ask for personal information or money.

- Don't Share Personal Information: Only share personal information over the phone if you're sure the caller is legitimate. If in doubt, hang up and call the organization directly using a trusted number.

- Call Blocking: Use call blocking features on your phone to block unknown or suspicious numbers.

Protecting Your Devices

In addition to recognizing and avoiding scams, protecting your devices is essential. Here are some tips for keeping your computers, smartphones, and tablets secure:

1. Use Strong Passwords and Encryption

Strong passwords and encryption help protect your devices and data from unauthorized access.

- Strong Passwords: Use strong, unique passwords for each device. Avoid using easily guessable information, like your name or birthday.

- Encryption: Enable Encryption on your devices to protect your data. Most modern devices have built-in encryption features.

2. Keep Your Software Updated

Updating your software is crucial for protecting your devices from the latest security threats.

- Automatic Updates: Enable automatic updates to ensure your operating system, antivirus software, and other programs are always up to date.

- Regular Checks: Regularly check for updates and install them promptly.

3. Use Security Software

Security software, such as antivirus and anti-malware programs, can help protect your devices from malicious software.

- Regular Scans: Run regular scans to detect and remove malware from your devices.

- Real-Time Protection: Enable real-time protection to prevent malware from being installed on your devices.

4. Secure Your Network

Securing your home network helps protect all the devices connected to it.

- Strong Wi-Fi Password: Use a strong password to protect your Wi-Fi network. Avoid using easily guessable passwords, like "password" or "123456."

- Network Encryption: Use WPA3 encryption for your Wi-Fi network. This is the latest and most secure encryption standard.

- Change Default Settings: Change your router's default username and password. Hackers often target default settings to gain access to networks.

5. Be Cautious with Public Wi-Fi

Public Wi-Fi networks can be less secure than your home network. Here's how to stay safe when using public Wi-Fi:

- Avoid Sensitive Activities: Avoid using public Wi-Fi for sensitive activities, like online banking or shopping.

- Use a VPN: Use a virtual private network (VPN) to encrypt your connection when using public Wi-Fi. This helps protect your data from being intercepted.

6. Back Up Your Data

Regularly backing up your data helps protect against data loss due to malware, hardware failure, or other issues.

- External Hard Drive: An external hard drive will back up your essential files. Keep the hard drive in a safe place.

- Cloud Storage: Use a cloud storage service to back up your files online. Choose a reputable service with solid security features.

By recognizing and avoiding scams, practicing safe communication, and protecting your devices, you can significantly reduce the risk of falling victim to cybercriminals. Cybersecurity is an ongoing process; staying vigilant is critical to securing your digital life.

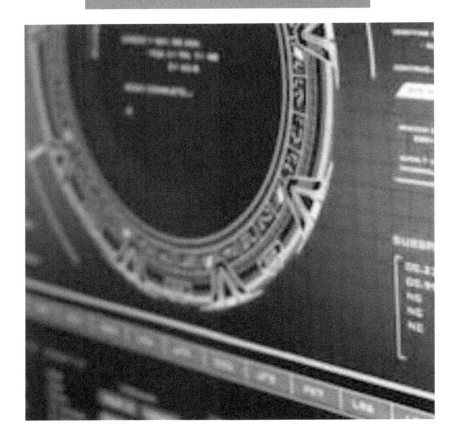

Chapter 5

Understanding Malware and Protecting Your Devices

Welcome to another chapter of this book! In this chapter, we'll look in-depth at malware, one of the most common threats in the digital world. We'll explore different types of malware, how they can affect your devices, and how to protect yourself against them. Let's dive in!

What is Malware?

Malware is short for "malicious software." It refers to software designed to harm, exploit, or otherwise compromise your computer, network, or device. Cybercriminals use malware to steal information, spy on your activities, and even take control of your devices.

Types of Malware

There are many types of malware, each with its methods and goals. Here are some of the most common types:

1. Viruses

A virus is a malware that attaches itself to a legitimate file or program. When you open the infected file, the virus spreads to other files and programs on your computer, causing damage.

- How Viruses Spread: Viruses can spread through email attachments, infected websites, or by sharing infected files through USB drives or other media.

- Effects of Viruses: Viruses can delete files, steal information, and slow down your computer. Some viruses are designed to cause as much damage as possible, while others are more subtle.

2. Worms

Worms are similar to viruses but don't need to attach themselves to a file. Instead, they spread through networks, infecting multiple computers.

- How Worms Spread: Worms can spread through email, instant messaging, or by exploiting vulnerabilities in software.

- Effects of Worms: Worms can cause significant damage by consuming bandwidth, deleting files, and installing other types of malware.

3. Trojans

Named after the Trojan Horse from Greek mythology, a Trojan is a type of malware that disguises itself as a legitimate program. Once you install it, the Trojan can steal your information or give hackers access to your computer.

- How Trojans Spread: Trojans often spread through email attachments, downloads from untrusted websites, or by pretending to be helpful software.

- Effects of Trojans: Trojans can steal personal information, install other malware, and give hackers remote access to your computer.

4. Ransomware

Ransomware is malware that locks your files or entire computer, demanding a ransom to unlock them. It's like a digital kidnapping of your data.

- How Ransomware Spreads: Ransomware often spreads through phishing emails, malicious websites, or by exploiting vulnerabilities in software.

- Effects of Ransomware: Ransomware can encrypt your files, making them inaccessible until you pay the Ransom. Even if you pay, there's no guarantee you'll get your files back.

5. Spyware

Spyware is malware that secretly monitors your computer activity and collects information without your knowledge. It can track your keystrokes, capture screenshots, and even record your browsing history.

- How Spyware Spreads: Spyware can spread through email attachments, malicious websites, or by being bundled with other software.

- Effects of Spyware: Spyware can steal personal information, monitor online activities, and slow down your computer.

6. Adware

Adware is a type of malware that displays unwanted advertisements on your computer. It can also track your browsing habits to show you targeted ads.

- How Adware Spreads: Adware often comes bundled with free software or through malicious websites.

- Effects of Adware: Adware can be annoying and intrusive, displaying pop-up ads and slowing down your computer.

7. Rootkits

Rootkits are malware that allows hackers to gain control of your computer without being detected. They can hide other malware and enable hackers to maintain access to your system.

- How Rootkits Spread: Rootkits can spread through email attachments, malicious websites, or by exploiting vulnerabilities in software.

- Effects of Rootkits: Rootkits can hide other malware, give hackers remote access to your computer, and be challenging to detect and remove.

How Malware Can Affect Your Devices

Malware can have a wide range of effects on your devices, from minor annoyances to severe damage. Here are some of the ways malware can affect your devices:

1. Slowing Down Your Computer

Malware can consume a lot of your computer's resources, causing it to slow down. You might notice that your computer takes longer to start up, programs run more slowly, or your internet connection could be faster than usual.

2. Stealing Personal Information

Many malware are designed to steal personal information, such as usernames, passwords, and credit card details. This information can be used for identity theft, financial fraud, or sold on the dark web.

3. Deleting or Corrupting Files

Some types of malware can delete or corrupt your files, causing you to lose important data. This can include documents, photos, videos, and other files.

4. Spying on Your Activities

Spyware and other types of malware can monitor your activities, capturing your keystrokes, screenshots, and browsing history. This information can be used to steal your identity, financial information, or other sensitive data.

5. Taking Control of Your Computer

Some types of malware, such as Trojans and rootkits, can give hackers remote access to your computer. They can use your computer to send spam emails, launch attacks on other computers, or steal your information.

6. Displaying Unwanted Advertisements

Adware can display unwanted advertisements on your computer, often in the form of pop-up ads. These ads can be annoying and intrusive, and they can also slow down your computer.

7. Demanding Ransom

Ransomware can lock your files or entire computer, demanding a ransom to unlock them. This can be very stressful and costly, and there is no guarantee that paying the Ransom will get your files back.

How to Protect Yourself from Malware

Protecting yourself from malware is crucial for keeping your devices and personal information safe. Here are some steps you can take to protect yourself:

1. Use Antivirus and Anti-Malware Software

Antivirus and anti-malware software can help detect and remove malicious programs from your computer. Keep your antivirus software current and run regular scans to check for threats.

- Regular Scans: Run regular scans to detect and remove malware from your computer.

- Real-Time Protection: Enable real-time protection to prevent malware from being installed on your computer.

- Update Definitions: Keep your antivirus software's definitions current to protect against the latest threats.

2. Keep Your Software Updated

Software updates often include security patches that fix vulnerabilities. Keeping your operating system, web browser, antivirus software, and other programs up to date can help protect against malware.

- Enable Automatic Updates: Enable automatic updates to ensure your software is always up to date.

- Check for Updates Regularly: Regularly check for updates and install them promptly.

3. Be Cautious with Email Attachments and Links

Be cautious about clicking links and downloading attachments from emails and messages, especially from unknown senders. Scammers often use email to spread malware.

- Verify the Sender: Check the sender's information to ensure the email is from a legitimate source.

- Hover Over Links: Hover over links to see the URL before clicking. If the URL looks suspicious, don't click.

- Scan Attachments: Use antivirus software to scan attachments before opening them.

4. Download from Trusted Sources

Only download files and programs from trusted sources. Avoid downloading anything from unknown or suspicious websites.

- Official Websites: Download software from the official website of the company that makes it.

- Trusted Repositories: Use trusted repositories and app stores to download software.

- Avoid Pirated Software: Pirated software is often bundled with malware. Avoid downloading or using pirated software.

5. Use a Firewall

A firewall helps block unauthorized access to your computer. Make sure your firewall is enabled and properly configured.

- Enable Firewall: Ensure your firewall is enabled in your operating system's settings.

- Configure Firewall: Configure your firewall to block unauthorized access and monitor incoming and outgoing traffic.

6. Back Up Your Data

Regularly backing up your essential files helps protect against data loss due to malware, hardware failure, or other issues.

- External Hard Drive: An external hard drive will back up your files. Keep the hard drive in a safe place.

- Cloud Storage: Use a cloud storage service to back up your files online. Choose a reputable service with solid security features.

7. Educate Yourself and Others

Stay informed about the latest cybersecurity threats and best practices. Please share your knowledge with friends and family to help them stay safe.

- Learn About Malware: Regularly read about new types of malware and cybersecurity threats.

- Share Information: Educate your friends and family about recognizing and avoiding malware.

Responding to Malware Infections

Even with the best precautions, you might still encounter malware. Here's how to respond if you think your device has been infected:

1. Disconnect from the Internet

If you suspect your device is infected with malware, disconnect from the Internet to prevent it from spreading or communicating with its creator.

- Turn Off Wi-Fi: Turn off your Wi-Fi connection or disconnect the Ethernet cable.

- Disable Bluetooth: Disable Bluetooth to prevent the malware from spreading to other devices.

2. Run a Malware Scan

Use your antivirus or anti-malware software to run an entire device scan. This can help detect and remove the malware.

- Full Scan: Run a full device scan to check for malware.

- Follow Instructions: Follow the instructions provided by your antivirus software to remove any detected threats.

3. Update Your Software

Make sure your operating system and all your software are up to date. This can help fix any vulnerabilities that the malware might have exploited.

- Install Updates: Install any available updates for your operating system and software.

- Enable Automatic Updates: Enable automatic updates to ensure your software is always up to date.

4. Change Your Passwords

If you think your device has been compromised, change your passwords immediately. This can help protect your accounts from being accessed by cybercriminals.

- Create Strong Passwords: Create strong, unique passwords for each account.

- Enable Two-Factor Authentication: Enable two-factor authentication (2FA) on your important accounts to add an extra layer of security.

5. Restore from Backup

If the malware has caused significant damage to your files, you should restore your files from a backup. Clean your device of malware before restoring your files to avoid reinfection.

- Clean Your Device: Ensure your device is malware-free before restoring your files.

- Restore Files: Restore your files from a recent backup. Use an external hard drive or cloud storage to retrieve your files.

6. Seek Professional Help

If you cannot remove the malware or are unsure what to do, seek professional help. A cybersecurity expert can help you remove the malware and secure your device.

- Contact a Professional: Contact a cybersecurity professional or a trusted tech support service.

- Explain the Issue: Provide as much information as possible to help the professional diagnose and fix the problem.

Advanced Malware Protection Techniques

In addition to the basic steps for protecting yourself from malware, there are some advanced techniques you can use to enhance your security:

1. Use a Virtual Private Network (VPN)

A VPN encrypts your internet connection, making it more difficult for cybercriminals to intercept your data. This can help protect your information when using public Wi-Fi or other untrusted networks.

- Choose a Reputable VPN: Choose a reputable VPN service with solid Encryption and a no-logs policy.

- Enable VPN: Enable the VPN when using public Wi-Fi or other untrusted networks to protect your data.

2. Use Sandboxing

Sandboxing is a security technique that isolates programs and processes from the rest of your system. This can help prevent malware from spreading or accessing sensitive information.

- Enable Sandboxing: Use software that supports sandboxing to run programs in isolated environments.

- Limit Permissions: Limit the permissions of programs and processes to minimize the risk of malware accessing sensitive information.

3. Use Intrusion Detection and Prevention Systems (I.D.P.S.)

I.D.P.S. can help detect and prevent unauthorized access to your network. These systems monitor network traffic for suspicious activity and can block potential threats.

- Install I.D.P.S.: Install an I.D.P.S. to monitor your network for suspicious activity.

- Configure I.D.P.S.: Configure the I.D.P.S. to block unauthorized access and alert you to potential threats.

4. Implement Network Segmentation

Network segmentation involves dividing your network into smaller segments to limit the spread of malware. This can help contain infections and protect sensitive information.

- Segment Your Network: Divide your network into smaller segments based on function or security level.

- Implement Access Controls: Use access controls to limit segment communication and protect sensitive information.

5. Use Endpoint Detection and Response (E.D.R.)

E.D.R. solutions provide continuous monitoring and analysis of endpoint devices to detect and respond to threats. This can help identify and mitigate malware infections quickly.

- Install E.D.R.: Install an E.D.R. solution on your endpoint devices to monitor for threats.

- Analyze Threats: Use the E.D.R. solution to analyze and respond to potential threats in real-time.

Understanding malware and how to protect yourself against it is crucial to cybersecurity. You can significantly reduce the risk of malware infections by using antivirus software, keeping your software updated, being cautious with email attachments and downloads, and following best practices for securing your devices. Cybersecurity is an ongoing process; staying vigilant is critical to securing your digital life.

Data Privacy and Protecting

Chapter 6

Data Privacy and Protecting Your Online Identity

This chapter will explore the importance of data privacy and how you can protect your online identity. With so much of our lives happening online, it's crucial to understand how to keep your personal information safe and secure. Let's get started!

What is Data Privacy?

Data privacy is all about protecting your personal information from being shared or accessed without your permission. It involves ensuring that your data is only accessible to you and the people you trust.

Why is Data Privacy Important?

Data privacy is essential for several reasons:

1. Protecting Personal Information

Your personal information is valuable and can be used for identity theft, financial fraud, and other malicious activities. Protecting your data helps prevent cybercriminals from accessing and using your information.

2. Maintaining Privacy

Everyone has a right to Privacy in the real world and online. Data privacy helps ensure your personal information remains private and isn't shared without your consent.

3. Preventing Financial Loss

Cybercriminals can use your personal information to commit financial fraud, such as opening bank accounts or making unauthorized purchases. Protecting your data helps prevent economic loss and other negative consequences.

4. Building Trust

When you protect your data, you help build trust with the people and organizations you interact with online. This is especially important for businesses and organizations that handle sensitive customer information.

How to Protect Your Data Privacy

Protecting your data privacy involves several steps and best practices. Here are some tips to help you keep your personal information safe:

1. Use Strong Passwords and Two-Factor Authentication

Using strong passwords and enabling two-factor authentication (2FA) can help protect your accounts from being compromised.

- Strong Passwords: Create strong, unique passwords for each account. Use a mix of letters, numbers, and special characters.

- Two-Factor Authentication: Enable 2FA on your important accounts to add an extra layer of security.

2. Limit the Information You Share

Be mindful of the information you share online, especially on social media and other public platforms.

- Privacy Settings: Use the privacy settings on social media to control who can see your information and posts. Only share with people you trust.

- Think Before You Share: Always consider whether the information you share is necessary and who will see it.

3. Use Encryption

Encryption helps protect your data by making it unreadable to anyone who intercepts it.

- Encrypt Your Device: Many smartphones and computers have built-in encryption features. Enable Encryption in your device's settings to protect your data.

- Use Encrypted Messaging Apps: Use messaging apps that offer end-to-end Encryption, like Signal or WhatsApp, to protect your conversations.

4. Be Cautious with Public Wi-Fi

Public Wi-Fi networks can be less secure than your home network. Here's how to stay safe when using public Wi-Fi:

- Avoid Sensitive Activities: Avoid using public Wi-Fi for sensitive activities, like online banking or shopping.

- Use a VPN: Use a virtual private network (VPN) to encrypt your connection when using public Wi-Fi. This helps protect your data from being intercepted.

5. Monitor Your Accounts

Regularly monitor your accounts for any suspicious activity. If you notice any unauthorized transactions or changes, report them immediately.

- Bank Accounts: Monitor your bank accounts and credit card statements for unauthorized transactions.

- Online Accounts: Check your online accounts for suspicious activity like password changes or new devices.

6. Use Privacy-Focused Tools

There are several tools and services available that can help protect your data privacy.

- Privacy-Focused Browsers: Use browsers that prioritize Privacy, such as Firefox or Brave. These browsers offer features like tracking protection and private browsing.

- Ad Blockers: Use ad blockers to prevent tracking scripts from collecting information about your browsing habits.

- Password Managers: Use password managers to create and store strong, unique passwords for each account.

7. Educate Yourself and Others

Stay informed about the latest data privacy threats and best practices. Please share your knowledge with friends and family to help them stay safe.

- Learn About Data Privacy: Regularly read about new data privacy threats and cybersecurity practices.

- Share Information: Educate your friends and family about how to protect their data privacy.

Protecting Your Online Identity

In addition to protecting your data privacy, it's essential to protect your online identity. Here are some steps you can take to keep your online identity safe:

1. Be Careful with Social Media

Social media is a great way to stay connected with friends, but it's also a common target for cybercriminals. Here's how to stay safe:

- Privacy Settings: Use the privacy settings on social media to control who can see your information and posts. Only share with people you trust.

- Avoid Oversharing: Don't share personal information like your address, phone number, or passwords. Be mindful of what you post and who can see it.

- Recognize Fake Profiles: Be cautious of friend requests from people you don't know. Fake profiles can be used to gather personal information or send harmful links.

2. Use Secure Email Practices

Email is another common target for cybercriminals. Here's how to stay safe:

- Check the Sender: Always check where the email is from. Be cautious if you don't recognize the sender or the email address looks strange.

- Avoid Clicking on Links: Don't click on links or download attachments from unknown or suspicious emails. They could lead to dangerous websites or download malware.

- Use a Secure Email Provider: An email provider offering robust security features, such as Gmail or Proton-Mail.

3. Protect Your Financial Information

Financial information is precious to cybercriminals. Here's how to protect it:

- Use Secure Payment Methods: Use secure payment methods, like credit cards or trusted payment services, when shopping online. Avoid using debit cards or direct bank transfers.

- Monitor Your Accounts: Regularly monitor your bank accounts and credit card statements for unauthorized transactions.

- Avoid Sharing Financial Information: Don't share your financial information, such as your bank account number or credit card details, unless necessary.

4. Be Cautious with Online Shopping

Online shopping is convenient, but it's essential to do it safely. Here are some tips:

- Shop on Trusted Websites: Only shop on websites you know and trust. Look for "https://" in the URL and a padlock icon to ensure the site is secure.

- Use Secure Payment Methods: Use secure payment methods, like credit cards or trusted payment services. Avoid using debit cards or direct bank transfers.

- Keep Your Information Private: Don't share unnecessary personal information. Only provide what's needed to complete your purchase.

5. Monitor Your Online Presence

Regularly monitor your online presence to check for any suspicious activity or unauthorized use of your information.

- Search for Your Name: Periodically search for your name online to see what information is available about you.

- Check Social-Media: Review your social media profiles to ensure your information is accurate and private.

- Use Alerts: Set up alerts for your name or other personal information to be notified of any new mentions or activity.

6. Use Identity Theft Protection Services

Identity theft protection services can help monitor your personal information and alert you to suspicious activity.

- Choose a Reputable Service: Choose a reputable identity theft protection service that offers comprehensive monitoring and protection.

- Review Alerts: Regularly review alerts from the service and take action if you notice any suspicious activity.

Responding to Identity Theft

Even with the best precautions, you might still become a victim of identity theft. Here's how to respond if you think your identity has been stolen:

1. Report the Theft

Report the identity theft to the appropriate authorities, such as your bank, credit card company, or a government agency.

- Contact Your Bank: Contact your bank or credit card company to report the theft and freeze your accounts.

- File a Report: File a report with a government agency, such as the Federal Trade Commission (F.T.C.) or the police.

2. Change Your Passwords

Change the passwords for your online accounts immediately to prevent unauthorized access.

- Create Strong Passwords: Create strong, unique passwords for each account.

- Enable Two-Factor Authentication: Enable two-factor authentication (2FA) on your important accounts to add an extra layer of security.

3. Monitor Your Accounts

Keep an eye on your accounts for any suspicious activity. If you notice any unauthorized transactions or changes, report them immediately.

- Bank Accounts: Monitor your bank accounts and credit card statements for unauthorized transactions.

- Online Accounts: Check your online accounts for suspicious activity like password changes or new devices.

4. Place a Fraud Alert

Place a fraud alert on your credit reports to make it harder for cybercriminals to open new accounts in your name.

- Contact Credit Bureaus: Contact the major credit bureaus (Equifax, Experian, and TransUnion) to place a fraud alert on your credit reports.

- Renew the Alert: Fraud alerts typically last 90 days but can be renewed if necessary.

5. Consider a Credit Freeze

A credit freeze can help protect your credit by preventing new accounts from opening in your name. This can be a more effective measure than a fraud alert.

- Contact Credit Bureaus: Contact the major credit bureaus to place a credit freeze on your credit reports.

- Lift the Freeze: You can lift the freeze temporarily or permanently if you need to apply for credit.

6. Review Your Credit Reports

Regularly review your credit reports to check for suspicious activity or unauthorized accounts.

- Request Reports: Request free copies of your credit reports from the major credit bureaus.

- Check for Errors: Review your reports for any errors or unauthorized accounts and report them to the credit bureau.

Safe Communication Practices

Communication is a big part of our online lives, and staying safe is essential. Here are some tips for safe communication:

1. Email Safety

Emails are a common way for scammers to try and trick you. Here's how to stay safe when using email:

- Check the Sender: Always check who the email is from. Be cautious if you don't recognize the sender or the email address looks strange.

- Avoid Clicking on Links: Don't click on links or download attachments from unknown or suspicious emails. They could lead to dangerous websites or download malware.

- Look for Red Flags: Watch out for emails that ask for personal information or have spelling and grammar mistakes. If something doesn't seem right, it isn't.

2. Social Media Safety

Social media is a great way to stay connected with friends, but keeping safe is essential. Here are some tips:

- Privacy Settings: Use the privacy settings on social media to control who can see your information and posts. Only share with people you trust.

- Be Careful What You Share: Don't share personal information like your address, phone number, or passwords. Be mindful of what you post and who can see it.

- Recognize Fake Profiles: Be cautious of friend requests from people you don't know. Fake profiles can be used to gather personal information or send harmful links.

3. Messaging Apps

Messaging apps are convenient for staying in touch with friends and family, but scammers can also use them. Here's how to stay safe:

- Use Encrypted Apps: Use messaging apps that offer end-to-end Encryption, like Signal or WhatsApp, to protect your conversations.

- Verify Contacts: If you receive a message from someone you don't know, verify their identity before responding. Be cautious of messages that ask for personal information or money.

- Avoid Suspicious Links: Don't click on links from unknown or suspicious messages. They could lead to dangerous websites or download malware.

4. Phone Calls

Phone calls are another standard method used by scammers. Here's how to stay safe:

- Verify the Caller: If you receive a call from an unknown number, verify the caller's identity before sharing any information. Be cautious of calls that ask for personal information or money.

- Don't Share Personal Information: Only share personal information over the phone if you're sure the caller is legitimate. If in doubt, hang up and call the organization directly using a trusted number.

- Call Blocking: Use call blocking features on your phone to block unknown or suspicious numbers.

Protecting Your Devices

In addition to protecting your data privacy and online identity, protecting your devices is essential. Here are some tips for keeping your computers, smartphones, and tablets secure:

1. Use Strong Passwords and Encryption

Strong passwords and encryption help protect your devices and data from unauthorized access.

- Strong Passwords: Use strong, unique passwords for each device. Avoid using easily guessable information, like your name or birthday.

- Encryption: Enable Encryption on your devices to protect your data. Most modern devices have built-in encryption features.

2. Keep Your Software Updated

Updating your software is crucial for protecting your devices from the latest security threats.

- Automatic Updates: Enable automatic updates to ensure your operating system, antivirus software, and other programs are always up to date.

- Regular Checks: Regularly check for updates and install them promptly.

3. Use Security Software

Security software, such as antivirus and anti-malware programs, can help protect your devices from malicious software.

- Regular Scans: Run regular scans to detect and remove malware from your devices.

- Real-Time Protection: Enable real-time protection to prevent malware from being installed on your devices.

4. Secure Your Network

Securing your home network helps protect all the devices connected to it.

- Strong Wi-Fi Password: Use a strong password to protect your Wi-Fi network. Avoid using easily guessable passwords, like "password" or "123456."

- Network Encryption: Use WPA3 encryption for your Wi-Fi network. This is the latest and most secure encryption standard.

- Change Default Settings: Change your router's default username and password. Hackers often target default settings to gain access to networks.

5. Be Cautious with Public Wi-Fi

Public Wi-Fi networks can be less secure than your home network. Here's how to stay safe when using public Wi-Fi:

- Avoid Sensitive Activities: Avoid using public Wi-Fi for sensitive activities, like online banking or shopping.

- Use a VPN: Use a virtual private network (VPN) to encrypt your connection when using public Wi-Fi. This helps protect your data from being intercepted.

6. Back Up Your Data

Regularly backing up your data helps protect against data loss due to malware, hardware failure, or other issues.

- External Hard Drive: An external hard drive will back up your essential files. Keep the hard drive in a safe place.

- Cloud Storage: Use a cloud storage service to back up your files online. Choose a reputable service with solid security features.

Responding to Device Compromises, even with the best precautions, your devices

It might still be compromised. Here's how to respond if you think your device has been compromised:

1. Disconnect from the Internet

If you suspect your device is compromised, disconnect from the Internet to prevent the malware from spreading or communicating with its creator.

- Turn Off Wi-Fi: Turn off your Wi-Fi connection or disconnect the Ethernet cable.

- Disable Bluetooth: Disable Bluetooth to prevent the malware from spreading to other devices.

2. Run a Malware Scan

Use your antivirus or anti-malware software to run an entire device scan. This can help detect and remove the malware.

- Full Scan: Run a full device scan to check for malware.

- Follow Instructions: Follow the instructions provided by your antivirus software to remove any detected threats.

3. Update Your Software

Make sure your operating system and all your software are up to date. This can help fix any vulnerabilities that the malware might have exploited.

- Install Updates: Install any available updates for your operating system and software.

- Enable Automatic Updates: Enable automatic updates to ensure your software is always up to date.

4. Change Your Passwords

If you think your device has been compromised, change your passwords immediately. This can help protect your accounts from being accessed by cybercriminals.

- Create Strong Passwords: Create strong, unique passwords for each account.

- Enable Two-Factor Authentication: Enable two-factor authentication (2FA) on your important accounts to add an extra layer of security.

5. Restore from Backup

If the malware has caused significant damage to your files, you might need to restore your files from a backup. Clean your device of malware before restoring your files to avoid reinfection.

- Clean Your Device: Ensure your device is malware-free before restoring your files.

- Restore Files: Restore your files from a recent backup. Use an external hard drive or cloud storage to retrieve your files.

6. Seek Professional Help

If you cannot remove the malware or are unsure what to do, seek professional help. A cybersecurity expert can help you remove the malware and secure your device.

- Contact a Professional: Contact a cybersecurity professional or a trusted tech support service.

- Explain the Issue: Provide as much information as possible to help the professional diagnose and fix the problem.

Advanced-Data Privacy and Protection Techniques

In addition to the basic steps for protecting your data privacy and online identity, there are some advanced techniques you can use to enhance your security:

1. Use a Virtual Private Network (VPN)

A VPN encrypts your internet connection, making it more difficult for cybercriminals to intercept your data. This can help protect your information when using public Wi-Fi or other untrusted networks.

- Choose a Reputable VPN: Choose a reputable VPN service with solid Encryption and a no-logs policy.

- Enable VPN: Enable the VPN when using public Wi-Fi or other untrusted networks to protect your data.

2. Use Sandboxing

Sandboxing is a security technique that isolates programs and processes from the rest of your system. This can help prevent malware from spreading or accessing sensitive information.

- Enable Sandboxing: Use software that supports sandboxing to run programs in isolated environments.

- Limit Permissions: Limit the permissions of programs and processes to minimize the risk of malware accessing sensitive information.

3. Use Intrusion Detection and Prevention Systems (I.D.P.S.)

I.D.P.S. can help detect and prevent unauthorized access to your network. These systems monitor network traffic for suspicious activity and can block potential threats.

- Install I.D.P.S.: Install an I.D.P.S. to monitor your network for suspicious activity.

- Configure I.D.P.S.: Configure the I.D.P.S. to block unauthorized access and alert you to potential threats.

4. Implement Network Segmentation

Network segmentation involves dividing your network into smaller segments to limit the spread of malware. This can help contain infections and protect sensitive information.

- Segment Your Network: Divide your network into smaller segments based on function or security level.

- Implement Access Controls: Use access controls to limit segment communication and protect sensitive information.

5. Use Endpoint Detection and Response (E.D.R.)

E.D.R. solutions provide continuous monitoring and analysis of endpoint devices to detect and respond to threats. This can help identify and mitigate malware infections quickly.

- Install E.D.R.: Install an E.D.R. solution on your endpoint devices to monitor for threats.

- Analyze Threats: Use the E.D.R. solution to analyze and respond to potential threats in real-time.

Understanding data privacy and how to protect your online identity is crucial to cybersecurity. By using strong passwords, limiting the information you share, using Encryption, being cautious with public Wi-Fi, monitoring your accounts, and using privacy-focused tools, you can significantly reduce the risk of your personal information being accessed or stolen. Cybersecurity is an ongoing process; staying vigilant is critical to securing your digital life.

We've covered a lot of ground in this chapter, but there's still much more to learn about cybersecurity. In the following chapters, we'll dive deeper into protecting your online identity, understanding the importance of software updates, and safe online communication practices. Together, we'll build the skills and knowledge you need to navigate the digital world safely and confidently. So, let's keep going and continue our journey into the world of cybersecurity!

Chapter 7

Protecting Your Online Identity

This new chapter, we'll explore the importance of protecting your online identity and how you can take steps to keep your personal information safe in the digital world. With more of our lives being lived online, it's crucial to understand how to safeguard your online identity. Let's get started!

What is Online Identity?

Your online identity is a collection of information about you that exists on the Internet. This can include your personal information, social media profiles, online accounts, and any other data associated with you online.

Why is Protecting Your Online Identity Important?

Protecting your online identity is essential for several reasons:

1. Preventing Identity Theft

Cybercriminals can use your personal information to steal your identity, which can lead to financial fraud, damaged credit, and other serious consequences. Protecting your online identity helps prevent identity theft.

2. Maintaining Privacy

Everyone has a right to Privacy in the real world and online. Protecting your online identity helps ensure your personal information remains private and isn't shared without your consent.

3. Avoiding Financial Loss

Cybercriminals can use your personal information to commit financial fraud, such as opening bank accounts or making unauthorized purchases. Protecting your online identity helps prevent economic loss and other negative consequences.

4. Building Trust

When you protect your online identity, you help build trust with the people and organizations you interact with online. This is especially important for businesses and organizations that handle sensitive customer information.

How to Protect Your Online Identity

Protecting your online identity involves several steps and best practices. Here are some tips to help you keep your personal information safe:

1. Use Strong Passwords and Two-Factor Authentication

Using strong passwords and enabling two-factor authentication (2FA) can help protect your accounts from being compromised.

- Strong Passwords: Create strong, unique passwords for each account. Use a mix of letters, numbers, and special characters.

- Two-Factor Authentication: Enable 2FA on your important accounts to add an extra layer of security.

2. Limit the Information You Share

Be mindful of the information you share online, especially on social media and other public platforms.

- Privacy Settings: Use the privacy settings on social media to control who can see your information and posts. Only share with people you trust.

- Think Before You Share: Always consider whether the information you share is necessary and who will see it.

3. Use Encryption

Encryption helps protect your data by making it unreadable to anyone who intercepts it.

- Encrypt Your Device: Many smartphones and computers have built-in encryption features. Enable Encryption in your device's settings to protect your data.

- Use Encrypted Messaging Apps: Use messaging apps that offer end-to-end Encryption, like Signal or WhatsApp, to protect your conversations.

4. Be Cautious with Public Wi-Fi

Public Wi-Fi networks can be less secure than your home network. Here's how to stay safe when using public Wi-Fi:

- Avoid Sensitive Activities: Avoid using public Wi-Fi for sensitive activities, like online banking or shopping.

- Use a VPN: Use a virtual private network (VPN) to encrypt your connection when using public Wi-Fi. This helps protect your data from being intercepted.

5. Monitor Your Accounts

Regularly monitor your accounts for any suspicious activity. If you notice any unauthorized transactions or changes, report them immediately.

- Bank Accounts: Monitor your bank accounts and credit card statements for unauthorized transactions.

- Online Accounts: Check your online accounts for suspicious activity like password changes or new devices.

6. Use Privacy-Focused Tools

There are several tools and services available that can help protect your online identity.

- Privacy-Focused Browsers: Use browsers that prioritize Privacy, such as Firefox or Brave. These browsers offer features like tracking protection and private browsing.

- Ad Blockers: Use ad blockers to prevent tracking scripts from collecting information about your browsing habits.

- Password Managers: Use password managers to create and store strong, unique passwords for each account.

7. Educate Yourself and Others

Stay informed about the latest online identity threats and best practices. Share your knowledge with friends and family to help them stay safe.

- Learn About Online Identity Protection: Regularly read about new online identity threats and cybersecurity practices.

- Share Information: Educate your friends and family about how to protect their online identity.

Responding to Online Identity Theft even with the best precautions:

You might still become a victim of online identity theft. Here's how to respond if you think your online identity has been stolen:

1. Report the Theft

Report the online identity theft to the appropriate authorities, such as your bank, credit card company, or a government agency.

- Contact Your Bank: Contact your bank or credit card company to report the theft and freeze your accounts.

- File a Report: File a report with a government agency, such as the Federal Trade Commission (F.T.C.) or the police.

2. Change Your Passwords

Change the passwords for your online accounts immediately to prevent unauthorized access.

- Create Strong Passwords: Create strong, unique passwords for each account.

-Enable Two-Factor Authentication: Enable two-factor authentication (2FA) on your important accounts to add an extra layer of security.

3. Monitor Your Accounts

Keep an eye on your accounts for any suspicious activity. If you notice any unauthorized transactions or changes, report them immediately.

- Bank Accounts: Monitor your bank accounts and credit card statements for unauthorized transactions.

- Online Accounts: Check your online accounts for suspicious activity like password changes or new devices.

4. Place a Fraud Alert

Place a fraud alert on your credit reports to make it harder for cybercriminals to open new accounts in your name.

- Contact Credit Bureaus: Contact the major credit bureaus (Equifax, Experian, and TransUnion) to place a fraud alert on your credit reports.

- Renew the Alert: Fraud alerts typically last 90 days but can be renewed if necessary.

5. Consider a Credit Freeze

A credit freeze can help protect your credit by preventing new accounts from opening in your name. This can be a more effective measure than a fraud alert.

- Contact Credit Bureaus: Contact the major credit bureaus to place a credit freeze on your credit reports.

- Lift the Freeze: You can lift the freeze temporarily or permanently if you need to apply for credit.

6. Review Your Credit Reports

Regularly review your credit reports to check for suspicious activity or unauthorized accounts.

- Request Reports: Request free copies of your credit reports from the major credit bureaus.

- Check for Errors: Review your reports for any errors or unauthorized accounts and report them to the credit bureau.

Protecting your online identity is a crucial part of cybersecurity. By using strong passwords, limiting the information you share, using Encryption, being cautious with public Wi-Fi, monitoring your accounts, and using privacy-focused tools, you can significantly reduce the risk of your personal information being accessed or stolen. Cybersecurity is an ongoing process; staying vigilant is critical to securing your digital life.

We've covered a lot of ground in this chapter, but there's still much more to learn about cybersecurity. In the following chapters, we'll dive deeper into specific topics like understanding the importance of software updates, safe online communication practices, and protecting your data privacy. Together, we'll build the skills and knowledge you need to navigate the digital world safely and confidently. So, let's keep going and continue our journey into the world of cybersecurity!

Chapter 8

The Importance of Software Updates

Welcome to Chapter 8! This chapter will explore the importance of keeping your software current. Software updates are crucial for maintaining the security and functionality of your devices. Let's dive in and learn why updating your software is essential and how to stay on top of it.

Why Are Software Updates Important?

Software updates are essential for several reasons:

1. Security

One of the primary reasons for software updates is to improve security. Cybercriminals are constantly looking for vulnerabilities in software that they can exploit. Software updates often include security patches that fix these vulnerabilities and protect your devices from being compromised.

- Fixing Vulnerabilities: Updates fix security holes that could be exploited by malware or hackers.

- Improving Defense: Updates can enhance security features and improve your device's ability to defend against threats.

2. Bug Fixes

Software updates often include fixes for bugs and other issues that can affect the performance and stability of your device. Keeping your software updated helps ensure your device runs smoothly and efficiently.

- Fixing Bugs: Updates address bugs and other issues that can cause your software to crash or behave unexpectedly.

- Improving Stability: Updates improve the stability and performance of your software, making it run more smoothly.

3. New Features

Software updates can also include new features and improvements that enhance the functionality of your device. By keeping your software up to date, you can take advantage of these new features and get the most out of your device.

- New Features: Updates can introduce new features and functionalities that improve user experience.

- Enhancements: Updates can improve existing features and make them more efficient and user-friendly.

4. Compatibility

Keeping your software up to date helps ensure it remains compatible with other software and devices. This is especially important for applications that rely on different software or hardware to function correctly.

- Compatibility with New Devices: Updates ensure your software remains compatible with new devices and technologies.

- Interoperability: Updates improve the ability of your software to work seamlessly with other applications and systems.

How to Stay on Top of Software Updates

Staying on top of software updates is crucial for maintaining the security and functionality of your devices. Here are some tips to help you keep your software up to date:

1. Enable Automatic Updates

Most operating systems and applications offer the option to enable automatic updates. This ensures that your software is always up to date without you having to remember to check for updates manually.

- Operating System: Enable automatic updates to ensure your operating system stays up to date with the latest security patches and improvements.

- Applications: Enable automatic updates for your applications to keep them current with the latest features and bug fixes.

2. Check for Updates Regularly

In addition to enabling automatic updates, checking for updates manually regularly is a good idea. This ensures you don't miss any important updates that might not be installed automatically.

- Operating System: Check for updates to your operating system regularly to ensure it stays current.

- Applications: Check for updates to your applications regularly to ensure they remain current.

3. Update Your Software Promptly

When you receive a notification about a software update, install it immediately. Delaying updates can leave your device vulnerable to security threats and performance issues.

- Install Updates Promptly: Install updates as soon as they become available to ensure your device remains secure and up to date.

- Avoid Delays: Avoid delaying updates, as this can leave your device vulnerable to security threats.

4. Use Trusted Sources

Only download software updates from trusted sources, such as the official website of the software developer or the app store for your device. Avoid downloading updates from unknown or suspicious websites.

- Official Websites: Download updates from the official website of the software developer to ensure they are legitimate.

- App Stores: Use trusted app stores like the Apple App Store or Google Play Store to download application updates.

5. Stay Informed

Stay informed about the latest software updates and security patches for your devices. Follow the official channels of the software developers and subscribe to their newsletters or social media updates to stay current.

- Follow Developers: Follow the official software developers' channels to stay informed about the latest updates and security patches.

- Subscribe to Newsletters: Subscribe to newsletters or social media updates from software developers to receive notifications about new updates.

Responding to Software Update Issues

Sometimes, software updates can cause issues with your device or applications. Here's how to respond if you encounter problems after updating your software:

1. Restart Your Device

Restarting your device can often resolve issues that occur after a software update. This can help clear any temporary glitches and ensure the update is applied correctly.

- Restart Your Device: Restart your device to resolve any temporary glitches that might occur after an update.

- Clear Temporary Issues: Restarting your device can help clear any temporary performance issues.

2. Check for Additional Updates

Sometimes, issues can be resolved by installing additional updates released after the initial update. Check for any further updates and install them if available.

- Check for Additional Updates: Check for any additional updates that might resolve issues after the initial update.

- Install Additional Updates: Install any additional updates to ensure your device remains up-to-date and secure.

3. Restore from Backup

If the software update causes significant issues that cannot be resolved, you might need to restore your device from a backup. Clean your device of any problems before restoring your files to avoid reinfection.

- Clean Your Device: Ensure your device is free of issues before restoring your files from a backup.

- Restore Files: Restore your files from a recent backup to resolve any issues after the update.

4. Seek Professional Help

If you need help to resolve the issues, seek professional help. A cybersecurity expert or tech support professional can help diagnose and fix the problem.

- Contact a Professional: Reach out to a cybersecurity expert or tech support professional to help resolve issues after a software update.

- Explain the Issue: Provide as much information as possible to help the professional diagnose and fix the problem.

Advanced Software Update Practices

In addition to the basic steps for keeping your software up to date, there are some advanced practices you can use to enhance your security:

1. Use a Centralized Update Management System

If you have multiple devices or manage a network, a centralized update management system can help streamline the update process and ensure that all your devices stay current.

- Centralized Management: Use a centralized update management system to manage updates for multiple devices.

- Streamline Updates: Streamline the update process to ensure all devices stay updated with the latest security patches and improvements.

2. Test Updates in a Controlled Environment

Before deploying updates to all your devices, consider testing them in a controlled environment to identify potential issues. This can help prevent disruptions and ensure a smooth update process.

- Controlled Testing: Test updates in a controlled environment before deploying them to all your devices.

- Identify Issues: Identify and resolve any potential issues before deploying the updates.

3. Implement a Patch Management Policy

A patch management policy can help ensure that updates are applied consistently and promptly. This can help improve security and reduce the risk of vulnerabilities.

- Patch Management Policy: Implement a patch management policy to ensure updates are applied consistently and promptly.

- Improve Security: Improve security and reduce the risk of vulnerabilities by applying updates promptly.

4. Use Update Monitoring Tools

There are several tools available that can help monitor your devices for updates and ensure that they stay up to date. These tools can provide notifications about available updates and help automate the update process.

- Update Monitoring Tools: Use tools that monitor your devices for updates and provide notifications about available updates.

- Automate Updates: Automate the process to ensure your devices stay updated with the latest security patches and improvements.

Keeping your software up to date is a crucial part of cybersecurity. By enabling automatic updates, checking for updates regularly, using trusted sources, staying informed, and following best practices for managing updates, you can significantly reduce the risk of vulnerabilities and improve the security and functionality of your devices. Cybersecurity is an ongoing process, and staying vigilant is critical to securing your digital life.

We've covered a lot of ground in this chapter, but there's still much more to learn about cybersecurity. In the following chapters, we'll dive deeper into safe online communication practices, protecting your data privacy, and understanding the importance of backups. Together, we'll build the skills and knowledge you need to navigate the digital world safely and confidently. So, let's keep going and continue our journey into the world of cybersecurity!

Chapter 9

Safe Online Communication Practices

Another opportunity, we'll explore safe online communication practices. With so much of our online communication, it's essential to understand how to stay safe and protect your personal information. Let's dive in!

Email Safety

Emails are a common way for cybercriminals to try and trick you. Here's how to stay safe when using email:

1. Check the Sender

Always check who the email is from. Be cautious if you don't recognize the sender or the email address looks strange.

- Verify the Sender: Verify the sender's information to make sure the email is from a legitimate source.

- Be Cautious: Be cautious of emails from unknown or suspicious senders.

2. Avoid Clicking on Links

Don't click on links or download attachments from unknown or suspicious emails. They could lead to dangerous websites or download malware.

- Hover Over Links: Hover over links to see the URL before clicking. If the URL looks suspicious, don't click.

- Scan Attachments: Use antivirus software to scan attachments before opening them.

3. Look for Red Flags

Watch out for emails that ask for personal information or have spelling and grammar mistakes. If something doesn't seem right, it isn't.

- Spelling and Grammar Mistakes: Legitimate organizations usually proofread their messages. If you notice multiple mistakes, be cautious.

- Urgent Language: Scammers often create a sense of urgency to pressure you into acting quickly without thinking.

4. Use a Secure Email Provider

Use an email provider with robust security features like Gmail or ProtonMail.

- Choose a Secure Provider: Choose an email provider with solid security features to protect your communication.

- Enable Security Features: Enable security features, such as two-factor authentication (2FA), to add an extra layer of security.

Social Media Safety

Social media is a great way to stay connected with friends, but keeping safe is essential. Here are some tips:

1. Privacy Settings

Use the privacy settings on social media to control who can see your information and posts. Only share with people you trust.

- Adjust Privacy Settings: Adjust the privacy settings on your social media accounts to control who can see your information.

- Limit Sharing: Limit the information you share to only what's necessary.

2. Be Careful What You Share

Don't share personal information like your address, phone number, or passwords. Be mindful of what you post and who can see it.

- Avoid Oversharing: Avoid sharing personal information that could be used to identify or locate you.

- Think Before You Post: Consider who can see your posts and what information you share.

3. Recognize Fake Profiles

Be cautious of friend requests from people you don't know. Fake profiles can be used to gather personal information or send harmful links.

- Verify Friend Requests: Verify friend requests from people you don't know before accepting them.

- Be Cautious: Be cautious of profiles that seem fake or suspicious.

Messaging Apps

Messaging apps are convenient for staying in touch with friends and family, but scammers can also use them. Here's how to stay safe:

1. Use Encrypted Apps

Use messaging apps that offer end-to-end Encryption, like Signal or WhatsApp, to protect your conversations.

- Choose Encrypted Apps: Choose messaging apps that offer end-to-end Encryption to protect your communication.

- Enable Encryption: Ensure Encryption is enabled in the app's settings.

2. Verify Contacts

If you receive a message from someone you don't know, verify their identity before responding. Be cautious of messages that ask for personal information or money.

- Verify Contacts: Verify the identity of contacts you don't know before responding to their messages.

- Be Cautious: Be cautious of messages that ask for personal information or money.

3. Avoid Suspicious Links

Don't click on links from unknown or suspicious messages. They could lead to dangerous websites or download malware.

- Hover Over Links: Hover over links to see the URL before clicking. If the URL looks suspicious, don't click.

- Scan Links: Use tools to scan links for potential threats before clicking on them.

Phone Calls

Phone calls are another standard method used by scammers. Here's how to stay safe:

1. Verify the Caller

If you receive a call from an unknown number, verify the caller's identity before sharing any information. Be cautious of calls that ask for personal information or money.

- Verify the Caller: Verify the caller's identity before sharing any information.

- Be Cautious: Be cautious of calls that ask for personal information or money.

2. Don't Share Personal Information

Only share personal information over the phone if you know the caller is legitimate. If in doubt, hang up and call the organization directly using a trusted number.

- Avoid Sharing Information: Avoid sharing personal information over the phone unless you know the caller is legitimate.

- Call Back: Hang up and call the organization directly using a trusted number if you're unsure.

3. Use Call Blocking

Use call-blocking features on your phone to block unknown or suspicious numbers.

- Enable Call Blocking: Enable call blocking features on your phone to block unknown or suspicious numbers.

- Use Call Blocking Apps: Call-blocking apps filter out unwanted calls.

Safe online communication is a crucial part of cybersecurity. By following best practices for email, social media, messaging apps, and phone calls, you can significantly reduce the risk of falling victim to cybercriminals and keep your personal information safe. Cybersecurity is an ongoing process, and staying vigilant is critical to securing your digital life.

Chapter 10

Protecting Your Data Privacy

Now let explore the importance of data privacy and how you can protect your personal information online. With more of our lives being lived online, it's crucial to understand how to safeguard your data. Let's get started!

What is Data Privacy?

Data privacy is all about protecting your personal information from being shared or accessed without your permission. It involves ensuring that your data is only accessible to you and the people you trust.

Why is Data Privacy Important?

Data privacy is essential for several reasons:

1. Protecting Personal Information

Your personal information is valuable and can be used for identity theft, financial fraud, and other malicious activities. Protecting your data helps prevent cybercriminals from accessing and using your information.

2. Maintaining Privacy

Everyone has a right to Privacy in the real world and online. Data privacy helps ensure your personal information remains private and isn't shared without your consent.

3. Preventing Financial Loss

Cybercriminals can use your personal information to commit financial fraud, such as opening bank accounts or making unauthorized purchases. Protecting your data helps prevent economic loss and other negative consequences.

4. Building Trust

When you protect your data, you help build trust with the people and organizations you interact with online. This is especially important for businesses and organizations that handle sensitive customer information.

How to Protect Your Data Privacy

Protecting your data privacy

Involves several steps and best practices. Here are some tips to help you keep your personal information safe:

1. Use Strong Passwords and Two-Factor Authentication

Using strong passwords and enabling two-factor authentication (2FA) can help protect your accounts from being compromised.

- Strong Passwords: Create strong, unique passwords for each account. Use a mix of letters, numbers, and special characters.

- Two-Factor Authentication: Enable 2FA on your important accounts to add an extra layer of security.

2. Limit the Information You Share

Be mindful of the information you share online, especially on social media and other public platforms.

- Privacy Settings: Use the privacy settings on social media to control who can see your information and posts. Only share with people you trust.

- Think Before You Share: Always consider whether the information you share is necessary and who will see it.

3. Use Encryption

Encryption helps protect your data by making it unreadable to anyone who intercepts it.

- Encrypt Your Device: Many smartphones and computers have built-in encryption features. Enable Encryption in your device's settings to protect your data.

- Use Encrypted Messaging Apps: Use messaging apps that offer end-to-end Encryption, like Signal or WhatsApp, to protect your conversations.

4. Be Cautious with Public Wi-Fi

Public Wi-Fi networks can be less secure than your home network. Here's how to stay safe when using public Wi-Fi:

- Avoid Sensitive Activities: Avoid using public Wi-Fi for sensitive activities, like online banking or shopping.

- Use a VPN: Use a virtual private network (VPN) to encrypt your connection when using public Wi-Fi. This helps protect your data from being intercepted.

5. Monitor Your Accounts

Regularly monitor your accounts for any suspicious activity. If you notice any unauthorized transactions or changes, report them immediately.

- Bank Accounts: Monitor your bank accounts and credit card statements for unauthorized transactions.

- Online Accounts: Check your online accounts for suspicious activity like password changes or new devices.

6. Use Privacy-Focused Tools

There are several tools and services available that can help protect your data privacy.

- Privacy-Focused Browsers: Use browsers that prioritize Privacy, such as Firefox or Brave. These browsers offer features like tracking protection and private browsing.

- Ad Blockers: Use ad blockers to prevent tracking scripts from collecting information about your browsing habits.

- Password Managers: Use password managers to create and store strong, unique passwords for each account.

7. Educate Yourself and Others

Stay informed about the latest data privacy threats and best practices. Share your knowledge with friends and family to help them stay safe.

- Learn About Data Privacy: Regularly read about new data privacy threats and cybersecurity practices.

- Share Information: Educate your friends and family about how to protect their data privacy.

Responding to Data Privacy Breaches

Even with the best precautions, you might still become a victim of a data privacy breach. Here's how to respond if you think your data has been compromised:

1. Report the Breach

Report the data privacy breach to the appropriate authorities, such as your bank, credit card company, or a government agency.

- Contact Your Bank: Contact your bank or credit card company to report the breach and freeze your accounts.

- File a Report: File a report with a government agency, such as the Federal Trade Commission (F.T.C.) or the police.

2. Change Your Passwords

Change the passwords for your online accounts immediately to prevent unauthorized access.

- Create Strong Passwords: Create strong, unique passwords for each account.

- Enable Two-Factor Authentication: Enable two-factor authentication (2FA) on your important accounts to add an extra layer of security.

3. Monitor Your Accounts

Keep an eye on your accounts for any suspicious activity. If you notice any unauthorized transactions or changes, report them immediately.

- Bank Accounts: Monitor your bank accounts and credit card statements for unauthorized transactions.

- Online Accounts: Check your online accounts for suspicious activity like password changes or new devices.

4. Place a Fraud Alert

Place a fraud alert on your credit reports to make it harder for cybercriminals to open new accounts in your name.

- Contact Credit Bureaus: Contact the major credit bureaus (Equifax, Experian, and TransUnion) to place a fraud alert on your credit reports.

- Renew the Alert: Fraud alerts typically last 90 days but can be renewed if necessary.

5. Consider a Credit Freeze

A credit freeze can help protect your credit by preventing new accounts from opening in your name. This can be a more effective measure than a fraud alert.

- Contact Credit Bureaus: Contact the major credit bureaus to place a credit freeze on your credit reports.

- Lift the Freeze: You can lift the freeze temporarily or permanently if you need to apply for credit.

6. Review Your Credit Reports

Regularly review your credit reports to check for suspicious activity or unauthorized accounts.

- Request Reports: Request free copies of your credit reports from the major credit bureaus.

- Check for Errors: Review your reports for any errors or unauthorized accounts and report them to the credit bureau.

Advanced-Data Privacy Protection Techniques

In addition to the basic steps for protecting your data privacy, there are some advanced techniques you can use to enhance your security:

1. Use a Virtual Private Network (VPN)

A VPN encrypts your internet connection, making it more difficult for cybercriminals to intercept your data. This can help protect your information when using public Wi-Fi or other untrusted networks.

- Choose a Reputable VPN: Choose a reputable VPN service with solid Encryption and a no-logs policy.

- Enable VPN: Enable the VPN when using public Wi-Fi or other untrusted networks to protect your data.

2. Use Privacy-Focused Search Engines

Privacy-focused search engines like DuckDuckGo do not track your search history or collect personal information. This can help protect your data privacy while browsing the internet.

- Choose a Privacy-Focused Search Engine: Use a search engine that prioritizes Privacy and does not track your searches.

- Avoid Tracking: Avoid using search engines that track your search history and collect personal information.

3. Use Secure Messaging Apps

Use messaging apps that offer end-to-end Encryption to protect your conversations. This ensures that only you and the person you're communicating can read the messages.

- Choose Secure Apps: Use messaging apps that offer end-to-end Encryption, such as Signal or WhatsApp.

- Enable Encryption: Ensure Encryption is enabled in the app's settings to protect your conversations.

4. Use Secure Cloud Storage

When storing files online, use a secure cloud storage service with solid Encryption and data protection features.

- Choose a Secure Service: Use a cloud storage service with solid Encryption and data protection features.

- Encrypt Your Files: Encrypt your files before uploading them to the cloud to add an extra layer of protection.

5. Be Cautious with Browser Extensions

Browser extensions can enhance your browsing experience, but they can also pose a risk to your data privacy. Only install extensions from trusted sources and review their permissions carefully.

- Choose Trusted Extensions: Only install browser extensions from trusted sources and developers.

- Review Permissions: Review the permissions of extensions carefully to ensure they do not have access to unnecessary data.

Protecting your data privacy is a crucial part of cybersecurity. By using strong passwords, limiting the information you share, using Encryption, being cautious with public Wi-Fi, monitoring your accounts, and using privacy-focused tools, you can significantly reduce the risk of your personal information being accessed or stolen. Cybersecurity is an ongoing process, and staying vigilant is critical to securing your digital life.

Chapter 11

Understanding the Importance of Backups

This chapter will explore the importance of backups and how to protect your data from being lost or corrupted. Backing up your data is crucial to cybersecurity and can help ensure you don't lose important information. Let's get started!

What is a Backup?

A backup is a copy of your data stored in a different location from the original. This can include documents, photos, videos, and other files. Backups can be stored on external hard drives, cloud storage, or other devices.

Why Are Backups Important?

Backups are essential for several reasons:

1. Protecting Against Data Loss

Data loss can occur for many reasons, such as hardware failure, malware infections, accidental deletion, or natural disasters. A backup ensures you can recover your data if lost or corrupted.

2. Ransomware Protection

Ransomware is malware that locks your files and demands a ransom to unlock them. Having a backup allows you to restore your files without paying the ransom.

3. Hardware Failure

Hardware can fail unexpectedly, and you could lose important data if you don't have a backup. Regular backups help ensure you can recover your data in case of hardware failure.

4. Accidental Deletion

It's easy to accidentally delete files or overwrite essential data. Having a backup allows you to recover deleted or overwritten files.

5. Natural Disasters

Natural disasters like fires, floods, or earthquakes can destroy your computer and data.

. Storing backups in a different location helps protect your data from being lost in a disaster.

Types of Backups

There are several types of backups you can use to protect your data:

1. Full Backup

A full backup is a complete copy of all your data. It's the most comprehensive type of backup, but it can take a long time to create and requires a lot of storage space.

- Complete Copy: A full backup creates a complete copy of all your data.

- Storage Requirements: Full backups require a lot of storage space and can take a long time to create.

2. Incremental Backup

An incremental backup only saves the changes made since the last backup. This type of backup is faster and requires less storage space than a full backup.

- Changes Only: Incremental backups save only the changes made since the last backup.

- Efficiency: Incremental backups are faster and require less storage than full backups.

3. Differential Backup

A differential backup saves the changes made since the last full backup. It's more comprehensive than an incremental backup but requires more storage space.

- Since Last Full Backup: Differential backups save the changes made since the last full backup.

- Balance: Differential backups are more comprehensive than incremental backups but require more storage space.

4. Cloud Backup

Cloud backups store your data on remote servers provided by a cloud storage service. This type of backup is convenient and accessible from anywhere with an internet connection.

- Remote Storage: Cloud backups store your data on remote servers.

- Accessibility: Cloud backups are accessible from anywhere with an internet connection.

5. Local Backup

Local backups store your data on external hard drives, USB drives, or other storage devices. This type of backup is fast and doesn't require an internet connection.

- External Storage: Local backups store your data on external storage devices.

- Speed: Local backups are fast and don't require an internet connection.

How to Create and Manage Backups

Creating and managing backups is crucial for protecting your data. Here are some tips to help you create and manage backups:

1. Choose the Right Backup Method

Choose the backup method that best suits your needs. Consider factors like how much data you need to back up, how often you need to back up, and your storage preferences.

- Assess Your Needs: Assess your data backup needs and choose the best method.

- Consider Storage Preferences: Consider your storage preferences, such as local storage or cloud storage.

2. Schedule Regular Backups

Schedule regular backups to ensure that your data is always up to date. Consider how often your data changes and how critical it is to have the latest version.

- Regular Schedule: Schedule regular backups to keep your data current.

- Frequency: Consider the frequency of backups based on how often your data changes.

3. Test Your Backups

Regularly test your backups to ensure that they're working correctly and that you can restore your data if needed.

- Regular Testing: Test your backups regularly to ensure they work correctly.

- Restore Process: Practice restoring your data to make sure you know how to do it in case of an emergency.

4. Store Backups in Multiple Locations

Store your backups in multiple locations to protect against data loss due to hardware failure, natural disasters, or other issues.

- Multiple Locations: Store backups in multiple locations to protect against data loss.

- Redundancy: Ensure redundancy by storing backups in physical and remote locations.

5. Use Encryption

Encrypt your backups to protect your data from being accessed by unauthorized individuals.

- Encrypt Backups: Use Encryption to protect your backups from unauthorized access.

- Security: Ensure the security of your data by using robust encryption methods.

Responding to Data Loss

Even with the best precautions, you might still experience data loss. Here's how to respond if you lose your data:

1. Restore from Backup

If you have a backup, restore your data from the backup to recover your lost or corrupted files.

- Use Your Backup: Restore your data from your backup to recover lost or corrupted files.

- Follow Instructions: Follow the instructions provided by your backup software to restore your data.

2. Check for Additional Backups

If your initial backup is unavailable or incomplete, check for additional backups containing the needed data.

- Multiple Backups: Check for additional backups containing the needed data.

- Explore Options: Explore different backup sources to find the most complete version of your data.

3. Seek Professional Help

If you cannot recover your data independently, seek professional help. A data recovery expert can help you recover your lost or corrupted files.

- Contact a Professional: Contact a data recovery expert to help recover your lost or corrupted files.

- Provide Information: Provide as much information as possible about the data loss to help the professional diagnose and fix the problem.

Backing up your data is a crucial part of cybersecurity. You can significantly reduce the risk of data loss by choosing the correct backup method, scheduling regular backups, testing your backups, storing backups in multiple locations, and using encryption. Cybersecurity is an ongoing process, and staying vigilant is critical to securing your digital life.

Conclusion

Your Journey into Cybersecurity

Welcome to the conclusion part of your journey into the world of cybersecurity. This book has taken you through the essentials of protecting yourself and your data in the digital age. From understanding cybersecurity to learning about common threats and how to defend against them, you've gained the knowledge and skills to navigate the online world safely. Let's recap what we've learned and discuss how to continue building on this foundation to stay secure in an ever-evolving digital landscape.

Recap of Key Concepts

Understanding Cybersecurity

We started with an introduction to cybersecurity, understanding its importance and the basic principles that underpin it. Cybersecurity protects your devices, networks, and data from unauthorized access, attacks, and damage. The digital world offers tremendous opportunities, but it also comes with risks, which makes cybersecurity essential for everyone.

Recognizing Cyber Threats

You learned about various cyber threats, including viruses, worms, trojans, ransomware, spyware, and adware. Each type of malware has different characteristics and effects, but all aim to disrupt your digital life, steal your information, or harm your devices. Recognizing these threats is the first step in defending against them.

Protecting Personal Information

Protecting your personal information is crucial in the digital age. We discussed the importance of using strong passwords, enabling two-factor authentication, and being cautious about what information you share online. Personal data can be used for identity theft and other malicious activities, so keeping it secure is paramount.

Safe Browsing Practices

Safe browsing practices include using secure websites, avoiding clicking on unknown links, and being cautious with downloads. These habits help prevent malware infections and protect your data from being compromised. Always look for "https://" in the URL and a padlock icon in the address bar to ensure a website is secure.

Email and Social Media Safety

Emails and social media are common targets for cybercriminals. You learned to recognize phishing scams, avoid clicking suspicious links, and use privacy settings to control who can see your information. Being vigilant about the content you interact with and share online can significantly reduce your risk of falling victim to scams.

Securing Your Devices

Securing your devices involves:

- Using antivirus software.
- Keeping your software updated.
- Enabling firewalls.
- Being cautious with public Wi-Fi.

These measures help protect your devices from malware and unauthorized access. Regularly updating your software ensures you have the latest security patches and improvements.

Data Privacy and Online Identity Protection

Data privacy controls how your information is collected, used, and shared. We discussed the importance of using encryption, limiting the information you share, and using privacy-focused tools. Protecting your online identity helps prevent identity theft and maintains your privacy in the digital world.

The Importance of Backups

Backing up your data is essential to prevent data loss from hardware failure, malware, or accidental deletion. You learned about different types of backups, such as whole, incremental, differential, cloud, and local backups, and how to create and manage them effectively. Regular backups ensure you can recover your data in case of an emergency.

Building on Your Cybersecurity Foundation

Now that you have a solid understanding of cybersecurity basics, it's essential to continue building on this foundation. The digital landscape constantly changes, and staying informed about new threats and best practices is vital to maintaining security. Here are some steps to help you continue your cybersecurity journey:

Stay Informed

Cybersecurity is an ever-evolving field, with new threats and solutions emerging regularly. Stay informed by following reputable cybersecurity news sources, subscribing to newsletters, and participating in online communities. Keeping up with the latest trends and developments will help avoid potential threats.

Regularly Review and Update Your Security Practices

Regularly review your security practices to ensure they are up to date. This includes updating passwords, enabling two-factor authentication, and checking for software updates. Make it a habit to assess your security measures and improve as needed periodically.

Educate Others

Please share your knowledge with friends and family to help them stay safe online. Cybersecurity is a shared responsibility; educating others can help create a more secure digital environment. Offer to help them set up strong passwords, enable two-factor authentication, and understand the importance of regular software updates.

Practice Safe Online Behavior

Continue practicing safe online behavior by being cautious with emails, social media, and websites. Avoid clicking on unknown links, downloading files from untrusted sources, and sharing personal information unnecessarily. Developing good habits will help you avoid many common cybersecurity risks.

Use Advanced Security Tools

As you become more comfortable with basic cybersecurity practices, consider using advanced security tools to enhance your protection. This can include using a virtual private network (VPN), implementing network segmentation, and using endpoint detection and response (E.D.R.) solutions. These tools provide additional layers of security to protect your data and devices.

Participate in Cybersecurity Training

Consider participating in cybersecurity training programs or courses to deepen your understanding of the field. Many organizations offer online courses, webinars, and workshops that cover advanced topics and provide hands-on experience. Continuous learning will help you stay updated with the latest threats and best practices.

Support Cybersecurity Initiatives

Support initiatives that promote cybersecurity awareness and education. This can include participating in events like National Cybersecurity Awareness Month, volunteering with organizations that teach cybersecurity skills, and advocating for policies that enhance digital security. Supporting these initiatives helps create a more secure digital world for everyone.

Cybersecurity and the Future

The future of cybersecurity is both challenging and promising. As technology continues to advance, new opportunities and risks will emerge. Here are some trends and developments to watch for in the coming years:

Artificial Intelligence and Machine Learning

Artificial intelligence (A.I.) and machine learning (ML) transform cybersecurity by improving threat detection and response. These technologies can analyze vast amounts of data to identify patterns and anomalies that indicate potential threats. A.I. and ML will be crucial in developing more effective security solutions.

The Internet of Things (IoT)

The Internet of Things (IoT) is expanding rapidly, with more devices connected to the internet than ever before. While IoT devices offer convenience and new capabilities, they also present new security challenges. Ensuring the security of IoT devices and networks will be a critical focus for cybersecurity professionals.

Cloud Security

Securing cloud environments becomes increasingly important as more data and applications move to the cloud. Cloud security involves protecting data stored in the cloud, ensuring secure access, and maintaining compliance with regulations. Organizations will need to adopt robust cloud security practices to protect their assets.

Quantum Computing

Quantum computing has the potential to revolutionize many fields, including cybersecurity. However, it also presents new security challenges, as quantum computers could break current encryption methods. Researchers are working on developing quantum-resistant encryption to address these challenges.

Privacy and Data Protection Regulations

Governments worldwide are implementing new privacy and data protection regulations to address growing concerns about data security. Regulations like the General Data Protection Regulation (G.D.P.R.) in Europe and the California Consumer Privacy Act (C.C.P.A.) in the United States aim to protect individuals' privacy and hold organizations accountable for data security.

Cybersecurity Workforce Development

The demand for skilled cybersecurity professionals is increasing. Developing a strong cybersecurity workforce is essential to addressing the increasing complexity of cyber threats. This includes providing education and training opportunities, promoting diversity in the field, and supporting career development for cybersecurity professionals.

Collaboration and Information Sharing

Collaboration and information sharing among organizations, governments, and individuals are crucial for improving cybersecurity. Sharing threat intelligence, best practices, and lessons learned helps create a collective defense against cyber threats. Encouraging collaboration and communication will enhance overall security.

Take Home

Cybersecurity is a critical aspect of modern life, and staying informed and proactive is essential for protecting yourself and your data. This book has provided the foundational knowledge and skills to navigate the digital world safely. You can contribute to a more secure digital future by continuing to learn, practicing safe online behavior, and supporting cybersecurity initiatives.

Remember, cybersecurity is an ongoing journey, not a destination. As you move forward, stay curious, informed, and vigilant. The digital world offers incredible opportunities but requires careful navigation to ensure your safety and security.

Thank you for joining me on this journey into the world of cybersecurity. We can build a safer and more secure digital world for everyone. Stay safe, stay secure, and continue to explore the fascinating and ever-evolving field of cybersecurity.

Additional Resources

To help you continue your cybersecurity journey, here are some additional resources:

1. **Books**

- "Cybersecurity for Dummies" by Joseph Steinberg

- "The Art of Invisibility" by Kevin Mitnick

- "Hacking: The Art of Exploitation" by Jon Erickson

- "Cybersecurity and Cyberwar: What Everyone Needs to Know" by P.W. Singer and Allan Friedman

- "Setup Your Laptop for Novice" by John George

Online Courses

- **Coursera:** Offers various cybersecurity courses and specializations from top universities.

- **edX:** Provides cybersecurity courses from institutions like M.I.T. and Harvard.

- **Udemy:** Offers a wide range of cybersecurity courses, including practical and hands-on training.

- **Cybrary:** A free platform offering courses on different aspects of cybersecurity.

1. **Websites and Blogs**

- **Krebs on Security:** A cybersecurity expert, Brian Krebs' blog covers the latest cybercrime.

- **The Hacker News:** Updates cybersecurity news, trends, and threats.

- **Dark Reading:** Offers articles and insights on cybersecurity topics.

- **Cybersecurity Ventures:** A research company offering reports and resources on cybersecurity.

Government Resources

- **U.S. Department of Homeland Security:** Offers resources and information on cybersecurity.

Continue Learning

As we end our journey into cybersecurity, we must reflect on the key lessons we've learned and understand how to continue applying these principles to stay safe in the digital world. Cybersecurity is an ongoing process requiring constant vigilance, awareness, and adaptation. You can navigate the internet safely and confidently by embracing the knowledge and practices covered in this book.

Cybersecurity is a dynamic field, and there's always more to learn. Continue your education by taking online courses, attending workshops, and reading books and articles on cybersecurity.

Cybersecurity is an essential aspect of modern life, and understanding how to protect yourself and your data is more critical than ever. By embracing the knowledge and practices covered in this book, you're well-prepared to navigate the digital world safely and confidently.

Remember, cybersecurity is an ongoing journey. Stay vigilant, stay informed, and stay proactive. Together, we can create a safer digital environment for everyone.

Thank you for joining me on this journey into the world of cybersecurity. I hope you've found this book informative, engaging, and empowering. Keep learning, stay safe, and continue to make cybersecurity a priority in your digital life.

Let's Continue the Journey

While this book concludes here, your journey into cybersecurity continues. Keep exploring, learning, and applying the principles you've learned. The digital world constantly evolves, and staying ahead of cyber threats requires ongoing effort and dedication.

Stay safe, stay informed, and remember cybersecurity starts with you.